ACCLAIM FOR
GROWING AN ENGAGED CHURCH

"*Growing an Engaged Church* provides foundational principles and praxis that will inspire us to recover and strengthen communities gathered to be God's people. This is a rich resource that's sure to guide us in implementing the Bishops' Pastoral Letter on Stewardship."

— The Rev. Jan Kevin Schmidt, Pastor
Immaculate Heart of Mary Church
Cincinnati, Ohio

"I believe *Growing an Engaged Church* is a truly groundbreaking work. It should be a wake-up call and a beacon of hope for all who serve in ministry."

— Leisa Anslinger
Author of *Here Comes Everybody!*
Whole Community Catechesis in the Parish

"Based on sound research, *Growing an Engaged Church* shows how congregational leaders who focus their efforts on increasing members' sense of belonging end up with members who are not only engaged, but also more spiritually committed. I plan to teach courses with this excellent book."

— The Rev. Dr. Philip D.W. Krey, President
The Lutheran Theological Seminary at Philadelphia

"This book presents a revolutionary approach to growing a healthy congregation. Best of all, it teaches you how to make it happen — and how to measure the results!"

— Dr. Sam Rima, Director
Doctor of Ministry and Leadership Enrichment programs
Bethel Seminary, St. Paul, Minnesota, and author of
Overcoming the Dark Side of Leadership

"I dream of churches shining like bright cities on hills all across our land. This book gives church leaders actionable strategies for realizing that vision."

— Rodney Plunket, Senior Minister
Church of Christ at White Station
Memphis, Tennessee

GROWING AN ENGAGED CHURCH

HOW TO STOP "DOING CHURCH" AND START BEING THE CHURCH AGAIN

ALBERT L. WINSEMAN

GALLUP PRESS

GALLUP PRESS
1251 Avenue of the Americas
23rd Floor
New York, NY 10020

Library of Congress Control Number: 2007922032

ISBN: 978-1-59562-014-9

Third Printing: 2009

This book is dedicated to my late father,
the Rev. Dr. Albert W. Winseman Jr.,
who as a pastor and teacher lived his life in service to others.
Through his example, I learned the truth of his philosophy
that people are not means to be used toward a goal;
people are the goal.

CONTENTS

FOREWORD

ne of the clear signs of the times, as revealed by surveys, book sales, and other indicators, is the recent surge of interest in spiritual matters among the American people and an intense hunger for God. Congregations, however, are having only limited success in tapping into this new and widespread spiritual yearning.

Churches have been in serious decline for nearly 40 years, and increasingly are labeled as lifeless and outmoded. Some observers of the religious scene go so far as to predict a "churchless Christianity" in the decades ahead.

Any further weakening of the local church could have sobering consequences because churches and other faith communities represent the heart and soul of America. They form the basic infrastructure of our country. At church, people worship God, connect with fellow seekers, and become empowered to reach out to a hurting society. Churches are way stations for rest and renewal in a broken world.

The response of some religious leaders, both clergy and lay, to their churches' failure to thrive is virtually to give up trying to change the situation, concluding that churches are at the mercy of inexorable forces such as relativism, privatism, hedonism, and narcissism.

Other leaders indulge in guesswork or hunches, or respond by following predictable paths, such as adding new activities, in the hopes of building up membership and revitalizing their congregations. These leaders miss the mark in that they fail to gain any real sense of what is on their congregants' hearts and minds, and of what they seek in a church home.

The challenge of building and revitalizing a church in trouble is daunting, but the fact remains that a church can be just about as healthy and vibrant as lay and clergy leaders want it to be. There *are* answers.

The basic problem, writes Al Winseman in this compelling and insightful book, is that churches insist on "doing church" — adding activities and going through more of the usual motions — rather than *being* the Church: that is, building a congregation of dedicated and energized members who are growing spiritually and, at the same time, are reaching out in concern and service to the world.

The difference between failing churches and flourishing churches is that the latter have a high percentage of "engaged" congregants, Winseman contends. These are people who, as congregation or parish members, know what is expected of them, regularly have the opportunity to do what they do best, feel their spiritual needs are being met, and feel their opinions count. Those, along with several other important characteristics, create a strong personal bond between these individuals and their church.

In this book, Winseman moves from *description* (describing the research process and offering case histories) to *prescription* (prescribing ways to build engagement levels in churches).

The main business of faith communities in the Christian tradition is to build disciples, or followers, of Jesus Christ. Too often, discipleship is overlooked and taken for granted. Dallas Willard describes the lack of discipleship as "the elephant in the church." Gallup research at the foundation of this book shows that, with regard to making disciples and proclaiming the good news of Jesus Christ, engaged churches do a better job than other churches.

Ever since I entered the field of polling more than a half century ago, it has been my persistent desire to bring survey research to the cause of religion and faith communities by examining levels of religious belief, behavior, and knowledge among the American people. I have always wanted to learn as much as possible about how people are responding to God or a higher power in their lives. Over the years, I have worked with countless churches and other faith communities, advising them on topics to explore in surveys and how to conduct such surveys. This is why I am so enthusiastic about this book: It is based on extensive survey research; it starts at the right place; it follows the right sequence; and it asks the right questions, all relating to important engagement outcomes.

Winseman, the leader of this breakthrough effort to engage congregations and revitalize churches, is well prepared for the challenge. For more than a decade, he served as a church planter and also as senior pastor at one of the largest and most successful United Methodist churches in the nation. His deep desire is to help churches, through solid and well-directed survey research, become vehicles for life transformation. He has the head of a researcher and the heart of a pastor.

The historical role of the Church in the United States is indeed threatened. At this time of deep spiritual hunger, it is imperative that faith communities *be* the Church. They must seize the day and make a wholesale commitment to engage existing and prospective members. In doing so, they will build a warm and embracing home in which faith can deepen, flourish, and bring forth new fruit for our communities and our nation.

—George Gallup Jr.
Founding Chairman of the George H. Gallup
International Institute

INTRODUCTION:
A HEART ATTACK WAITING TO HAPPEN

I was participating in my denomination's yearly convention, which we United Methodists call our Annual Conference. Although I'm a clergy member of the Conference, I'm no longer a pastor of a local church, and my current work has sometimes prevented my attending. But last year, I wasn't speaking or consulting or leading seminars during Conference time, so I was looking forward to attending, renewing friendships, and participating in the business of the Conference — especially because the event was addressing some critical issues facing the churches in my state.

The details of those critical issues left me more than a little depressed. Here are just a few of the dispiriting things I learned:

- In 1970 (the year I was confirmed as a member of my United Methodist church), the lay membership in my Annual Conference was about 146,000. By 2004, that membership had plummeted *by nearly half* — to 84,000.

- During that same period, average weekly worship attendance *decreased by nearly a third.*

- In 2004, one-fourth of the United Methodist Churches in my Conference did not receive a single new member!

- The average age of a clergy member in ministry in my Conference is 54, and there are only four fully ordained clergy under 35.

- At the annual ordination service, only two full clergy members were ordained — and both of them were over 40.

I don't like hearing bad news — nobody docs! I served churches in my Annual Conference for 15 years, and the numbers above aren't just statistics to me. They represent personal stories. But the facts speak for themselves, and they aren't pretty. And it's even more distressing to note that if you were to substitute just about any region or denomination, you'd see similar trends.

Yet too often, we Christians choose to ignore or minimize the severity of the trouble we're in. Because we love the Church — or maybe because we're in denial — we tend to put on our rose-colored glasses and view the situation as we'd *like* it to be rather than how it actually *is*. This isn't surprising; it's true of most people in many situations. Sometimes, especially when it comes to the relationships and organizations we love, we don't take a long, hard, realistic look at problems.

I've made that mistake, and I'm sure you have, too. But wearing rose-colored glasses has not served Christians well in the last part of the 20th century and into the opening decade of the 21st, because U.S. congregations have been in serious decline for nearly 40 years.

Let me say it again: the Church in the United States is in serious trouble. All the warning signs are there. Some are more obvious than others. One ominous sign is that congregational membership as a proportion of the U.S. population is shrinking. It's true: *Congregational membership in the United States increased by almost 9% in the decade between 1990 and 2000. But the overall U.S. population increased by a little more than 13% during that same time.* Church membership growth is not keeping up with population growth; the Church is losing ground.

IGNORING A HEART CONDITION

A handful of leaders — but only a handful — have recognized the seriousness of the problem and are creatively taking necessary measures to address it. Many leaders see the warning signs and realize they are facing a major challenge, but don't know what to do; nothing seems to work anymore. Others see the signs and think if they just continue down the same path (in other words, if they don't change), things will eventually — magically — get better. Still others think nothing is wrong and go about their business as usual, oblivious to the dangers that lie ahead.

What if at-risk patients responded in this way to their doctors' warnings about a heart attack? With high cholesterol levels, precariously elevated blood pressure, 50 pounds of excess weight, and a sedentary lifestyle, these patients are in serious danger. If such patients were to say, "Thanks, doc, but I feel just fine. I don't see any need to change what I'm doing"; or to frantically try every health fad out there, hoping something would lead them to success; or to recognize the warning signs, but illogically think, "I'll just keep doing what I've always done, eat what I've always eaten, not change anything about my lifestyle, and in a few months I'll see some improvement in my health" — we'd call such responses foolish at best.

Yet many churches are following precisely this logic when it comes to their spiritual health. Doing the same thing again and again, and expecting different results — didn't Einstein define that as insanity?

It's gone far beyond shortness-of-breath-while-climbing-the-stairs for most segments of the Church in America. The vast majority of mainline Protestant churches are experiencing serious chest pains on a regular basis; those churches are massive heart attacks waiting to happen. It's time for major surgery and a radical lifestyle change.

Why? Because the Presbyterians, Methodists, Disciples of Christ, United Church of Christ, Episcopalians, and most other denominations have seen steadily declining membership for more than the past quarter century; some denominations have diminished by nearly 50%. For example, in 1968, there were 11 million United Methodists in the United States attending 42,000 churches. By 2003, there were 8.1 million members in almost

35,000 churches. That's a drop-off during those 35 years of 26% in membership and 17% in the number of congregations.

For the Presbyterian Church (USA), the news is worse: In the same time frame, it has gone from 4 million members in more than 12,000 churches to 2.4 million members in 11,000 churches — a decline of 40% in membership and 8% in the number of congregations.

But the decline is hardly limited to mainline Protestants. Gallup Organization polling data show that the percentage of Americans who identify themselves as Southern Baptists has declined by more than half in the past decade: from 10% in 1995 to 4% in 2005. And despite the growth in megachurches over the past 20 years (which is real), the percentage of American Christians who choose no denominational affiliation has remained steady. So, we are not seeing real growth, but a reshuffling of the deck chairs on that famous, iceberg-bound ship.

Protestants aren't the only Christian faith group that is a coronary waiting to happen. Roman Catholics are in the midst of a severe shortage of priests that doesn't show signs of abating — and this was a crisis even before the sexual abuse scandals of the last few years broke into the news. What's more, despite the huge influx of immigrants in the past 20 years from Latin American countries that are predominantly Catholic, the percentage of Americans who identify themselves as Catholic has consistently remained about 25%.

ISN'T CHURCHLESS CHRISTIANITY A CONTRADICTION?

Amazingly, some leaders don't see the decline of the local church as a problem. In fact, they regard churchless Christianity as the next evolutionary step in the Christian faith, and they celebrate this new emphasis on the individual at the expense of the community. They tend to see the local church as a hindrance to an individual's spiritual growth, and they regard belonging to a local church as just one option among many for living a faithful Christian life — and not an attractive one at that. I think those who espouse and celebrate the supposed irrelevance of the local church are flat-out wrong — and Gallup data back up my claim. Church members tend to be *more* spiritually committed than nonmembers are.

I'll write in more detail about spiritual commitment and how to measure it in a subsequent chapter, but right now it's important to note that 18% of members of congregations are "fully spiritually committed" — compared with only 5% of nonmembers. To put it another way, church members are more than *three and a half times as likely* as nonmembers to be fully spiritually committed! This empirical evidence supports the Biblical wisdom found in the letter to the Hebrews: "And let us consider how to provoke one another to love and good deeds, not neglecting to meet together, as is the habit of some, but encouraging one another."

While it is possible for an individual to be spiritually committed without belonging to a congregation, it is difficult. Contrary to the claims of churchless Christianity, the local church is vital to an individual's spiritual formation. But churches can and must do better. They need to stop *doing church* and start *being the Church*. And the premise of this book is that being the Church requires a fundamental change in our thinking. I am a firm and enthusiastic believer in the local church, and agree with Willow Creek Community Church Pastor Bill Hybels whenever he states (and he does so often) that "the local church is the hope of the world." The phrase "individual Christian" truly is an oxymoron — the Christian faith is meant to be lived out in community, as Jesus modeled in his life together with his disciples. And with all its shortcomings and challenges (it is made up of human beings, after all!), it is still the local church that God has chosen as the vehicle through which Christ is made known to the world.

So if we believe the world is in need of the life-giving love of Jesus Christ, we'd better do everything we can not only to strengthen existing local congregations, but also to effectively plant new churches that meet the needs of and proclaim the Gospel to emerging generations. The two are not mutually exclusive.

Although I am a strong champion of the local church, this doesn't mean I unquestioningly support institutional Christianity. Nor do I give an uncritical blessing to everything local churches do. Many churches waste valuable resources devoting inordinate attention and energy to things that really don't advance the Kingdom of God; they major in the minors and completely miss ministry opportunities that would improve their spiritual health and enable them to reach people for Christ and the Church. And that is a tragedy.

Neither am I all that interested in helping the institution get well; in fact, institutional Christianity needs to be completely "re-formed" in order to better support the mission and ministry of local churches. That is the way it's been for nearly 2,000 years of Christianity: Institutional religion has crumbled, reformed, re-visioned, and even completely died off — but local congregations have remained. To be sure, congregations have changed over the centuries, but they have never ceased to exist; they are still God's Plan A for sharing the Gospel.

Now, a lot of congregations are too closely tied to institutional religion, and are simply going through the motions of "doing church." These churches and their leaders need to wake up before it's too late; they must start being in mission rather than maintenance. They need to realize that the Church is the only organization that exists for reasons other than its own self-preservation. Leaders must help their congregations *be* the Church. And in order to be the Church, congregations need to achieve and maintain an optimum level of spiritual health — which is much more easily said than done.

FROM DOING TO BEING

I wrote this book to help clergy and lay leaders focus on what's important to their churches' spiritual health. The principles and practices you will find in the following pages apply to all the various tribes of the Christian faith — be they Protestant,

Catholic, or Orthodox. I use the terms "church," "parish," "congregation," and "faith community" interchangeably, because whatever term is used in your tradition, it is the health of that base unit — the local church, parish, congregation, and so on — that is the critical issue.

The hope for fixing what's wrong with local churches isn't at the institutional level; in fact, the institution itself is frequently a source of the problem. Increasingly out of touch with contemporary culture (and with local congregations and their members!), these bureaucracies often seem to promote their own agendas at the expense of ministry at the local-church level. If the Church is to recover and thrive in the United States, it will be up to you — the pastors, lay leaders, and members of local churches — not the institutional Church. Institutional leaders should realize that their lives depend on healthy congregations. They should start doing all in their power to assist those congregations — or get out of the way.

To become healthy again, the Church needs to stop *doing* and start *being*. Now, when I say, "stop *doing*," I don't mean stop doing things like caring for the poor, feeding the hungry, sheltering the homeless, or any of the other ministries that the Church is called to pursue. Rather, the Church must stop focusing on institutional preservation. It must get back to the basics (particularly the basics found in the Acts of the Apostles) and rediscover what it means to *be* the church.

Part of being is being healthy. Doing church has made us sick — sick unto death. We are in a spiritual health crisis. This book provides diagnostic tools for measuring your congregation's spiritual health, and then taking steps to improve it.

We need to realize and find inspiration because, even in the midst of the crisis, Americans have continued to demonstrate that they are a religious and spiritual people. Indeed, according to some of the latest Gallup research, Americans seem to be more religious than they were 10 years ago. Ninety-four percent say they believe in God, 89% state a religious preference, 63% say they are members of a faith community, and 44% report they have attended a religious service in the past seven days. In addition, 59% say religion is very important in their lives, and 59% also report that religion can answer most of today's problems.

There is hope — not just among individuals but also among congregations. There are Protestant congregations that pulsate with life, have a *vibrant* spirit that's almost palpable, and are reaching out to and serving others in their communities and world with a passion that can be described only as miraculous. There are Catholic parishes that are alive and reaching out to new immigrants and making a real, tangible difference in their communities.

Why are some congregations and parishes flourishing while others are failing? What makes the difference?

The difference is *engagement*.

"GOOD SOIL" CHURCHES

A church with a high proportion of engaged members is like the good soil Jesus mentioned in the parable of the sower and the seed, found in the Gospels of Matthew, Mark, and Luke. In the parable, a sower goes out to sow some seed. Some fell along the path, some in the rocks, some among the thorns, and some in the good soil. For various reasons, the seed that fell in the rocks, along the path, and among the thorns eventually died, but the seed that fell in the good soil grew and produced "a hundredfold."

In his explanation to the disciples, Jesus says the seed represents "the word of God" and the various places where the seed landed represent the different responses people have to the word of God. The good soil represents those who hear the word and act on it, producing fruit. Engaged churches are "Good Soil" churches.

For millennia, farmers have been finding and implementing ways to improve soil conditions so they can grow more and better crops. They have used all of the methods at their disposal through the ages to produce more abundantly. But all of their scientific progress in soil preparation doesn't diminish the miracle of life. God's design of how life springs forth from a single seed, even though we can examine and describe the science behind it, remains an awesome wonder.

Measuring engagement, and implementing strategies to improve it, is just like preparing the soil to produce an abundant crop. It is no secret that there are some churches that produce abundant fruit of the Spirit; and there are others that seem as dry as a withered fig tree, bearing no fruit. Increasing engagement in your church is simply employing the latest research and discoveries — preparing the soil — so God can produce a bumper crop; it's creating a receptive climate for the work of the Holy Spirit, so God can do great things in your midst.

The secret to growing an engaged church is preparing the soil. The ultimate goal of the engaged congregation is to be a community of faith that is ready, willing, and able to respond to God's call and produce fruit — "thirty, sixty, a hundredfold." I pray this happens in your church, and I believe that what's presented in this book is in line with what God expects from the Church: to make disciples and proclaim the Good News of Jesus Christ. Engaged churches do that better than nonengaged or disengaged ones. Quite simply, improving engagement enables a church to better accomplish God's purpose for it.

Indeed, Gallup research demonstrates that congregations with engaged members are spiritually healthier, are better able to carry out their missions, attract more new people, are better able to fund new ventures, and have a higher percentage of spiritually committed individuals. In short, they are more effective than congregations with not-engaged or actively disengaged members.

The old ways of doing things just don't work anymore. If you find yourself nodding in agreement, you're a leader who is tired of shopworn methods that are trotted out, dressed up, given new names, and introduced as the Next Big Thing. You are frustrated with the conventional advice to "just copy the successful congregations, and you will be successful, too." You want real, workable, practical solutions to the problems you are facing in your congregation. This book turns the conventional wisdom upside down and offers new insights into how to solve your congregation's problems — and improve its spiritual health.

In the chapters ahead, you will be introduced to the critical concept of engagement and the importance of measuring it. Until now, religious leaders have had no way to determine the most relevant factors in congregational spiritual health, and thus have not been able to measure it — or manage it. Attempts have been made in the past several years to measure spiritual health, but because what was being measured had no credible link to relevant outcomes, these attempts were ineffective. In contrast, Gallup's research is demonstrably linked to relevant outcomes. As we examine the data, we will drill down deeper, uncovering Gallup's discoveries regarding the powerful connections that exist among spiritual commitment, congregational engagement, and the relevant outcomes of life satisfaction, inviting, serving, and giving.

So lay aside the conventional wisdom. You'll find that the discoveries in this book resonate with all you've intuitively known to be true about healthy congregations, and you'll have more than your share of "Aha!" moments. I know I did when researching and writing it. Now hang on tight, and prepare to be challenged.

CHAPTER ONE:
JEFF AND TRICIA'S SEARCH FOR A CHURCH

eff and Tricia are like just about everybody else on the planet: They have a God-sized hole in their lives.

But Jeff and Tricia are different from most Christians in the United States because they are aware of the hole. And they are even more unusual because at one time in their lives, that hole was filled.

The way Jeff and Tricia filled that hole was through their church. Every week as they participated in worship, they came away moved by the music, or the drama, or the "witness talks" by members, or the pastor's message. There wasn't a week when they didn't feel, at some time during worship, the presence of God. They came to like their church's more contemporary, thematic approach to worship — blending urban gospel and contemporary Christian music, using soloists backed up by a choir and a seven-piece band, drama that dealt with real-life issues, and relevant messages from the pastor, who rarely failed to make an emotional connection with most worshipers. The church was growing rapidly (one year, it nearly tripled its average worship attendance), and although there were many newcomers each week, Jeff and Tricia always felt the pastors and other leaders loved and cared for them. New members said there was a spirit about their church that set it apart from just about every other church in the city.

Their church supported many local and international ministries to the poor — Habitat for Humanity, food pantries, the American Cancer Society's Relay for Life, and Heifer Project International, to name but a few. One of Jeff and Tricia's favorite outreach ministries was their coordinating of Project Angel Tree, in which church members provided Christmas gifts for families of the inmates in the local prison.

Jeff and Tricia served their church gladly: Tricia was one of the best children's ministry leaders the church had, and Jeff served on the church's strategic mapping team and taught adult Bible classes. Their closest friends were members. Jeff and Tricia gave sacrificially, even finding a way to donate $20,000 to the building fund campaign over and above their regular tithe. They felt themselves to be growing spiritually, and discovered the "God-sized hole" in their lives was being filled.

Then Jeff was offered a promotion at work, which meant a transfer to a different city. The hardest part about moving away from the city they called home for seven years was leaving their church. They spent a lot of time discussing and praying about the situation, and eventually decided Jeff should take the promotion and they would move. Even though they were leaving a church family they loved, they thought they could eventually find a church home in their new city.

Little did they know how difficult it would be.

FEELING DISCONNECTED AND DISCOURAGED

After Jeff and Tricia got settled into their new home, they started "church shopping." The city they moved to was about a third the size of the one they left, so already there were fewer churches to choose from. They visited more than a dozen churches — most of them more than once. They visited churches of their own denomination, churches of other denominations, independent churches, churches that offered traditional worship, and churches that offered "boomer contemporary" worship. But throughout their search, they just didn't experience the emotional connection in worship they had felt in their former church.

Jeff and Tricia were in a quandary. But they were not about to give up yet.

During their year of church shopping, they noticed a new church building was going up just five minutes from where they lived. They watched the progress of construction with interest, because the church was a mainline denomination church that was relocating. When the building was completed, Jeff and Tricia decided to visit.

Their first visit was encouraging. The worship center was warm and inviting, and it was nearly filled to capacity. There was a band, a praise team leading singing, and words to the songs were projected on the screens. The preaching was good, too, and there seemed to be a lot of positive energy in the congregation. It wasn't exactly like their former church, but it was as close as they'd been in a long time. They decided to return.

Over the course of nearly a year, Jeff and Tricia attended the church regularly. But during that time, not once did anyone from the church personally contact them, even though they signed the attendance register each week. They did, however, get a letter inviting them to become members after their third Sunday in attendance — Tricia remembers that it seemed a bit presumptuous. But they kept attending anyway, trying to figure out ways to become involved.

The couple decided that a good way to get to know some of the members was to join a monthly dining-out group advertised in the church newsletter. They showed up at the restaurant and joined four other couples who obviously knew each other well. After they all introduced themselves, the couples who were already friends conversed about shared experiences, laughing and talking and having a great time — but nearly always excluding Jeff and Tricia. The same thing happened the next three months, even though Jeff and Tricia each tried numerous times to join the conversations. Not surprisingly, they stopped going to the dinners, figuring that no one would miss them anyway.

One Sunday, Jeff answered a call for volunteers to sing in a special choir for Ash Wednesday. He showed up for the first rehearsal, introduced himself to the choir's director, got some music, and joined the baritone section. The other choir members were polite, but not particularly welcoming. Yet Jeff kept coming to rehearsal the next three weeks, tried unsuccessfully to get to know others in the choir, and sang with the choir at all three Sunday morning services. It's a good thing Jeff enjoyed the singing, because the experience didn't otherwise make him feel wanted or needed.

Yet even with these discouraging experiences, the couple still decided to join the church. They were persistent, because the feeling of having that God-sized hole filled is not easily forgotten — and individuals will go to great lengths to have it filled once again. Jeff and Tricia thought that perhaps membership would unlock some doors for them.

So they signed up for "Coffee With the Pastors," which they anticipated would be a Q & A session, followed by an opportunity to enroll in membership classes. But to their surprise, Coffee With the Pastors was the only membership class offered: a two-hour Sunday afternoon session in which the prospective members introduced themselves, and the pastors talked about the history of the church, did a 30-minute overview of the Bible, and handed out a stack of information about the church — including a financial pledge card, a Spiritual Gifts Assessment, and a Ministry Opportunities Worksheet. The prospective new members were assigned sponsors, who would meet them before worship the next week, and were asked to complete the Spiritual Gifts Assessment, the Ministry Opportunities Worksheet, and the pledge card, and bring them all to the new-member dinner after the worship service.

So Jeff and Tricia dutifully filled out their forms — but not without a lot of head scratching. The 144 items on the Spiritual Gifts Assessment seemed to be directed to pastors or church professionals. These are some of the items Jeff and Tricia were asked to answer:

- Christians from outside of my normal ministry circle often seek out my advice.

- I am able to put other Christians to work using their gifts and talents.

- I proclaim God's message in a way especially effective for introducing Christ to those who do not know Him.

- I speak in tongues as a personal spiritual exercise.

- It seems important to share the truth of God's Word even if it irritates others.

- People have told me I was God's instrument that brought about supernatural change in lives or circumstances.

- It is quite natural for me to embody Biblical truths in my daily life.

- I have a clear understanding of Biblical doctrines.

- I can judge well between the truthfulness and error of a given theological statement.

"Wow," thought Tricia, "I wonder what people who haven't been in church that often would think of this? They'd probably be scared off!"

The Ministry Opportunities Worksheet wasn't much better — especially because no one took the time to explain the different ministries in which members could be involved. The form was confusing and listed names of ministries Jeff and Tricia didn't understand, like New Beginnings Home Volunteer, Personal Intercessor, Alpha-Omega Relay Captain, Loaves and Fishes, Joyful Journey Navigator, and Hang-Time Host Family — and the form didn't go into further detail about any of the ministries. Jeff and Tricia came away thinking there was a lot going on, but they had no basis for deciding what to be involved in or how to get involved.

On new-member Sunday, Jeff and Tricia showed up, met their sponsors, and came up to the front to be introduced, along with 42 other new members. After church, they went into the family life center for the new-member dinner. They went through the buffet line with their sponsors, ate dinner, and made small talk. The church staff was introduced and each staff member briefly described his or her ministry area, followed by the new members introducing themselves. The pastor said a prayer, and then they all went their separate ways to enjoy a pleasant Sunday afternoon.

And that was it — the sum total of Jeff and Tricia's new-member experience at the church. Oh, yes, they did receive a card from the volunteer coordinator, thanking them for joining and saying that if they ever wanted to get involved in a ministry, they should give her a call.

Jeff and Tricia still attend worship regularly, write a check each week (though for not nearly as much as they gave to their former church), but they don't feel particularly wanted, needed, or engaged. They've all but given up trying to fill that God-sized hole in their lives, thinking that maybe it was a once-in-a-lifetime experience — an experience they both cherish and long to discover once again.

A LUKEWARM CHURCH

If you're seeing your church in this story (and I don't mean the church Jeff and Tricia moved away from), you're not alone. Jeff and Tricia's experience is not at all unique; it is replicated all over the country in thousands of churches each week. People with God-sized holes in their lives show up, hoping beyond hope to get just a portion of that hole filled. But many of them walk away still carrying the void, and are more discouraged than when they first came.

This phenomenon is quite disturbing, considering the Biblical emphasis on the crucial role spiritually healthy churches play in reaching people for Christ and making disciples. Matthew's Gospel records Jesus as saying, "on this rock I will build my church," and while Bible scholars have debated the origin and meaning of these words for centuries — and probably will still argue them for centuries to come — one thing is clear: By placing these words on the lips of none other than Jesus himself, the Biblical witness declares the primary importance of the Church in the overall schema of the Christian faith.

The experience of so many churches today resembles another Biblical witness, this time from the book of Revelation. Now, it's always a little tricky to bring Revelation into any discussion because of the imagery John uses to describe Christ's eventual triumph over evil, but a scene in Revelation stands out because it is eerily descriptive of so many churches in America today. The third chapter of Revelation describes the risen and exalted Christ addressing seven churches in Asia Minor. To the church at Laodicea, Christ tells John to write:

I know your works; you are neither cold nor hot. I wish that you were either cold or hot. So, because you are lukewarm, and neither cold nor hot, I am about to spit you out of my mouth. For you say, "I am rich, I have prospered, and I need nothing." You do not realize that you are wretched, pitiable, poor, blind, and naked.

The church at Laodicea was complacent and self-satisfied — and also spiritually impoverished. Its lukewarm Christianity was unpalatable, and its members had lost their passion — their fire — for reaching others with the Gospel. They had stopped making disciples. They had ceased to be a movement and instead had become an institution.

Sadly, I am afraid many, many churches in the United States today fit this description — and they don't even realize they are lukewarm and unpalatable. Jeff and Tricia represent a best-case scenario for these churches, because people like them will stick it out anyway. But most people who encounter what Jeff and Tricia did will simply not come back, and will quietly slip away from the influence of any church.

In analyzing Jeff and Tricia's story, at least three things stand out that can help church leaders who are serious about not just *doing* church, but actually *being* the Church. Pay attention to these factors, and you'll reclaim the Biblical heritage of the Church found in Acts: a growing community of followers of Christ who were passionate about the message and mission of the new movement, who practiced radical hospitality, and who were so emotionally engaged with the movement that they were willing to risk everything to see it succeed.

WHY BE WELCOMING?

The first factor is that few people, if any, in their new church reached out to Jeff and Tricia to make them feel not just welcome, but wanted. Whenever people evaluate whether they want to belong to — or deepen their involvement in — an organization, they ask two questions: "Am I valued?" and "Do I make a meaningful contribution?" This is true of any organization, be it a workplace, a school, or a service club. But it is especially true of the Church. Jeff and Tricia's experience made them doubt they were valued, because no one reached out to them. The Spiritual Gifts Assessment, with its confusing verbiage, made them feel inadequate. And because no one took the time to find out about their talents and strengths, Jeff and Tricia didn't think they had anything of value to offer their new church.

The congregants that Jeff and Tricia had met at the church probably had been members for a long time, and naturally had common experiences that Jeff and Tricia did not share. That is a natural part of the life cycle of groups. After about 18 months, a group tends to become closed, in that the members now have a history together. Because of that shared history, it becomes difficult for new members to join such a group. Churches that are serious about making newcomers feel welcome in collective experiences are constantly forming new groups of new people — who can then create their own shared history.

But the problem at this church is deeper than just the particulars of group dynamics: Hospitality is obviously not one of the core congregational values. Although it may be one of the church's written values, it is not lived out. And that is a leadership issue.

Many leaders see hospitality as a strategy for growth rather than something that has intrinsic value. Jeff and Tricia's new church was a growing church — at least in terms of worship attendance. One benefit of its decision to move to a rapidly growing part of the city was a 30% increase in worship attendance during its first year in the new building. If the church was already growing, why should members go to the trouble of practicing hospitality and demonstrating an inviting spirit?

Well, without a spirit of hospitality, the church's numerical growth will probably be short-lived. Its worship may still attract a crowd, but if those who are coming don't feel valued or wanted, they will find their way out just as easily as they found their way in. Jeff and Tricia are probably prime candidates for leaving if they ever find a church that, in addition to the other qualities they are looking for, makes them feel both valued and that they can make a meaningful contribution.

THE VALUE OF MEMBERSHIP

A second factor that stands out is the church's new-member process—a process that is replicated at thousands of churches across the country. Several issues need to be addressed if membership is to have any meaning at all to those who are joining. First, it is problematic that membership classes consisted of only one two-hour meeting. Now, I'm not advocating that every church send inquirers through a two-year membership course (unless that fits your congregation and tradition), but I do recommend raising the bar a little. People can give their allegiance to myriad organizations; when they give it to your congregation, the time commitment you require for membership classes should reflect the value you place on membership. When leaders tell people that the only requirement for church membership is attendance at a two-hour orientation, they send those people the message that membership is not particularly important.

Another issue with the membership process is that Jeff and Tricia came away knowing only one thing that was expected of them as members: They received a pledge card, so they figured they were expected to give. But at no time did either pastors or staff members clarify the expectations of membership at the church. As you will see in a subsequent chapter, communicating and clarifying expectations are crucial to engaging members in your congregation.

Yet another issue with membership involved the Spiritual Gifts Assessment and the Ministry Opportunities Worksheet. One of the major problems with most spiritual gifts inventories (and there are a plethora of them — just Google "spiritual gifts inventory" and you'll see what I mean) is that they are filled with religious jargon that assumes the inventory taker has been involved in his or her church for years. Unchurched people or those who have not been particularly active in a church are often confused and intimidated by the language, and wind up discouraged. Distributing such a survey without spending time explaining and teaching about it typically has negative results.

There was a similar problem with the Ministry Opportunities Worksheet. No one explained any of the ministries to the new members; they were just turned loose to figure everything out on their own. No wonder Jeff and Tricia were confused! If you give new members such a worksheet and you expect people to serve in the ministries you list, you'd better explain them.

In the end, the new-member process for Jeff and Tricia reinforced, rather than alleviated, their feelings of not being valued and not being able to make a meaningful contribution to the congregation.

EMOTIONS MATTER

A third factor that stands out about Jeff and Tricia's experience is the prominence that making an emotional connection has in their — or anyone's — search for a church. This is an important part of belonging to a congregation or parish that is often ignored and more often misunderstood.

Most church leaders confuse involvement with engagement. They believe the conventional wisdom: The way to get new members to really connect with their new church is to get them involved in something — *any*thing! But involvement is not engagement. Involvement is what you *do* in and for your church; engagement is how you *feel* about your church. This is a crucial difference. Engagement is about emotions. Good Soil churches have a climate that fosters a deep and strong emotional connection.

Many observers of the changing religious scene in America see the decline of mainline churches and the growth of more conservative Protestant churches in the past 30 years and conclude that these trends have a predominantly theological explanation; they think the primary draw of conservative, evangelical churches is the theological and Biblical viewpoints they espouse. But our research doesn't support those conclusions. Let's dig deeper, and look at evangelical Christians in the United States.

In measuring the percentage of evangelical Christians, it is helpful to use some generally agreed-upon criteria; for a number of years, Gallup has used the following: 1) a "born again" experience, 2) belief in the Bible as the "actual word of God," and 3) belief in the responsibility to share one's faith with others. The percentage of Americans who meet these criteria has remained remarkably stable over the past 30 years at roughly 20%. Therefore, the increase in attendance at evangelical Protestant churches apparently isn't because of an increase in the number of people adhering to evangelical beliefs. But let's examine each of those criteria a little more closely.

First, let's look at beliefs about the Bible. If you go to the Web site of almost any conservative evangelical church, you will find in its statement of faith an affirmation that the Bible is the "actual Word of God, without error." However, the percentage of Americans who believe the Bible is the "actual word of God, to be taken literally, word for word" has declined remarkably: In 1963, 65% believed this, but that figure is now at 32%. More than likely, the increase in attendance at evangelical Protestant churches doesn't result from an increasing number of people who believe in the inerrancy of the Bible.

Second, let's look at faith sharing. In 1976, the first year The Gallup Poll asked whether respondents had "encouraged someone to believe in Jesus Christ, or accept Him as his or her Savior," 47% said they had. By 2005, that figure had risen slightly, to 52%. While it is impressive that a little more than half of the adults in the United States have shared their faith with someone, a 5-point increase over 30 years isn't really enough to account for the rise in attendance among evangelical churches.

Which brings us to the third criterion: a born-again experience. Gallup first asked about a born-again experience in 1976, when presidential candidate Jimmy Carter revealed he was a "born-again Christian." That year, 35% of the adults in the

United States said they had been "born again or had a born-again experience," a "turning point" in their lives when they committed themselves to Jesus Christ. By 2005, that figure had risen to 48% — nearly half of the adult population!

When you calculate the percentage of evangelicals according to the formula and compare the figures over time, you can see the total percentage has remained about the same. But what makes up the total has changed: Faith-sharing has remained fairly stable, literal belief in the Bible has dropped off, and the born-again experience has risen. And it is the born-again experience that is the key.

What is driving declining attendance in mainline Protestant churches and fueling the increasing attendance in conservative Protestant churches is not that people are holding to more conservative theological or Biblical beliefs. Our research suggests that it is mostly because of the critical but often overlooked importance of the emotional connection. Simply put, conservative churches have been doing a much better job at connecting with people at an emotional level than have mainline churches.

Neurological research confirms that our emotional connections are far stronger than our rational connections — it's not enough to know that belonging to an organization has positive benefits; one must also *feel* it. And more often than not, we feel it before we *know* it. Often, that initial emotional connection comes in the worship experience, which is why Jeff and Tricia were so keen on finding a worship experience that touched them. In today's postmodern world, people don't show up at worship services because they want to know more about God; they come because they want to *experience* God. They want to have an emotional connection with the holy.

That is where conservative evangelical churches typically beat mainline churches, hands down. For years, most mainline Protestant worship has been wary of emotion. Mainline leaders embraced modernity and its emphasis on the rational with great vigor; the greatest compliment a modern mainline preacher could get was, "Reverend, that sermon really made me *think*." In the postmodern world, the greatest compliment is, "Pastor, worship really *moved me* today." And scientific research confirms that the emotional bond is far stronger than the rational.

That's not to say intellectual integrity doesn't matter or that emotions should be manipulated in order to produce the desired feeling. But if members are to grow in their faith, they need to have established an emotional bond with their congregation. And for that bond to have optimum strength, it must go beyond just the worship experience.

In fact, the emotional bonds that have nothing to do with worship are even stronger. That's what engagement is, and that's why I wrote this book: to help you decode the emotional bonds that tie members to their churches and to each other. It is what Jeff and Tricia were searching for in a new church home, and they won't be fulfilled until they find it.

People just like Jeff and Tricia show up at your church every Sunday. Will you be ready to welcome them, and make them feel they are valued and have something meaningful to give? Are you "preparing the soil," so that when the Jeffs and Tricias decide to call your church their home, they can bear fruit? As you continue to read, you'll discover the keys to meeting their needs and empowering them for service.

CHAPTER TWO:
WHAT REALLY COUNTS

M any churches use surveys to find out what's on the minds of their congregants, particularly when they have an important decision to make or they want to evaluate a ministry or program. Unfortunately, most of those surveys have absolutely no linkage to any measurable outcomes. As such, their metrics are questionable at best. Put another way: If you can't measure it, you can't manage it.

This is true for all types of organizations that aspire to effectiveness and excellence. In their desire to measure and manage, leaders sometimes choose to measure issues that have no real bearing on an organization's effectiveness.

Take Robert's experience with his congregation's attempt at measurement.

Robert brings in his mail one evening after coming home from work. He notices an envelope from his church and opens it right away. It's the Annual Membership Survey, a list of 57 items (there were 48 last year) that he is asked to rate on a scale of 1 to 10. "Well, I guess I'll do it now and get it out of the way," he sighs as he sits down at the kitchen table.

Diligently filling out the survey, Robert comes to an item that says, "Our church does a good job of teaching the Bible." He ponders aloud, "Hmmm. I don't know. Maybe they do; maybe they don't. The pastor obviously mentions the Bible in his sermons every week, but other than that, I don't know what else is going on," and he circles a 3. Robert doesn't know that of the 2,000 members of his congregation, 800 participate in weekly small-group Bible studies, and those 800 consider their weekly study group an indispensable part of their lives.

The problem is not that Robert's church doesn't do a good job of teaching the Bible; it does. It's just that Robert doesn't know about the church's network of Bible studies, and so he *thinks* it doesn't do a particularly good job in that area.

The real problem, though, is with the survey itself: Each of the committee members who designed it had his or her own ideas about what constitutes an effective, growing church. One committee member thought a great music program was important, so he wanted to include questions about music. Friends of another committee member attended another church and raved about that church's children's programs, so the member wanted to include questions about children's ministries. Other committee members weren't too happy that the worship format for the 11 a.m. service had been changed from traditional to contemporary, so they included several questions to confirm their bias. Still another felt that the church's adult education program was its best feature, so she wanted to add some questions dealing with that. And so on.

The result of this process was a 57-item hodgepodge questionnaire that had no link to measurable outcomes.

If your measurement instrument has no link to outcomes, it isn't worth much to your congregation. And before you can design such an instrument, you must define your outcomes.

A CURSORY EXAMINATION

For my annual physical, suppose my doctor did a visual exam — telling me to "open wide and say 'ahhh,'" taking out his little hammer and testing my reflexes, looking in my ears and eyes, and poking and prodding in the all usual places. And then suppose he took measurements of only what was easiest to measure: my height, weight, and pulse rate. And then, after this short examination, he declared me to be in great health — although recommending that I lose 10 pounds or so. Would you consider this a thorough physical exam? Of course not! Where's the blood pressure check? The blood tests? The urinalysis? Where are the "measures that matter"?

Most churches determine their spiritual health in a similar way. They do a cursory examination (What shape is our building in? Do we like the music?) and then measure easy, basic stuff: membership, attendance, and giving.

"But wait a minute!" you might be saying. "Aren't membership, attendance, and giving the best measures of a church's success and effectiveness? After all, if they weren't the most important measures, why would congregational, denominational, and diocesan leaders put so much emphasis on them?"

Those are good questions. The second is easiest to answer, so let's get that one out of the way first. So much emphasis is placed on membership, attendance, and giving because these three outcomes are the easiest to measure. Nearly every church keeps a membership roll of some sort, counts the number of people who show up for worship or Mass each week, and tracks the money it receives. So it's pretty simple to monitor these items — they go up, go down, or stay the same from week to week, month to month, and year to year. But are they really the best indicators of your church's spiritual health? Let's take a look.

Membership. This seems like a pretty straightforward measure. Membership tells you who "signs up." If a congregation is healthy, it should be growing, right? If things are going well within a faith community, doesn't it stand to reason that more and more people would want to become members? Membership statistics appear to be relatively straightforward, but there is much, much more to them than meets the eye.

First of all, how do congregations count "membership"? Who qualifies as a member? Is it only adults aged 18 and older? Are new members required to take a class before joining? Or is just coming forward and saying "I want to be a member" enough? Are members required to meet standards for attendance, community service, and financial support? What about doctrinal standards? Is it easier to join the congregation than it is to be removed from the membership rolls?

Second, nearly every church has its share of "inactive" members. How many inactive members are on a congregation's membership rolls? How do those congregations deal with them? Do they stay on the rolls until they ask to be removed? Is showing up once or twice a year enough to maintain membership?

Third, what is known about the spiritual health of those on the membership rolls? Does membership guarantee spiritual growth? Or are there different levels of spiritual maturity among the members of each faith community?

Fourth, what is known about the neighborhood or larger community of which a congregation is a part? Is it growing or declining? In transition? Are there young families moving in or out? Are most members over 65? Under 40? Demographics can have a considerable impact on congregational membership that is totally unrelated to spiritual health.

Because each congregation handles membership differently — from its definition of membership, to who qualifies, to the membership requirements   and because membership doesn't reveal anything deeper than who claims to be a part of a congregation, membership statistics are not particularly helpful in measuring spiritual health. Those statistics do provide useful information, but not the information leaders need to shepherd their congregations effectively.

Attendance. This should be a better measure, right? Attendance tells you who "shows up." Counting those who attend Mass or worship services will tell you a lot about the spiritual health of a congregation — or so says the conventional wisdom. After all, people show up for services only if their faith is healthy and growing, don't they? Sort of.

It's true that individuals who are committed and engaged attend religious services more regularly than the uncommitted and disengaged do. But committed, engaged individuals are not the only ones coming to services. There are many other, less committed folks attending on an average Saturday or Sunday — or other days in some traditions. Attendance statistics record only that people are showing up for services. And if services are interesting and meaningful, more people will show up than will do so if they are boring.

Other factors influence attendance, too: What are the service times? What is the format — contemporary, traditional, blended? If there is music in the service, what's it like? And just as in membership, the demographic characteristics of the community have an impact on attendance.

Attendance is a more useful indicator of spiritual health than is membership — but not by much.

Giving. Giving tells you who "chips in." How much members give financially to their congregation is one of the more relevant indicators of the spiritual health of that congregation. Gallup research has discovered a decisive link between individuals' spiritual health levels and the amount of money they give to their congregations. Those who have a higher level of spiritual health (as determined by factors to be discussed at length in this book) tend to give more; those with a lower level tend to give less.

So if giving is the only relevant indicator, or outcome, of spiritual health among the "big three," are there any others? Yes there are.

THE FOUR RELEVANT OUTCOMES OF SPIRITUAL HEALTH

When Gallup started investigating spiritual health, we looked at many outcomes to see how accurately they indicated the level of spiritual health in a congregation. Through careful and thorough research, examination, and analysis, we discovered that four outcomes are the most accurate and relevant. Other outcomes may indicate something about a congregation's life, but like membership and attendance, they have little connection to the primary causes of spiritual health.

It is important to be clear about the outcomes, because they tell leaders whether they are "hitting the mark." It is also important to be clear about the differences between outcomes and causes, because most congregations and their leaders confuse the two — which is a disastrous mistake.

The four outcomes that are the most relevant indicators of a church's spiritual health are: life satisfaction, inviting, serving, and giving.

Life Satisfaction. Common sense tells us that people who are part of a spiritually healthy congregation should be more satisfied with their lives than are those who belong to no faith community or to an unhealthy congregation. According to the results of our research and analysis, this is indeed the case. In order to measure life satisfaction, we asked members of congregations to rate the following statement on a scale of 1 (strongly disagree) to 5 (strongly agree):

I am completely satisfied with my life.

Sixty-one percent of those who are engaged in their congregations strongly agree with this statement. This does not mean they are happy all the time or that they have known no sorrow or hardship in their lives. It does indicate that because they are part of healthy congregations, they are better able to cope with life's vicissitudes. They have a sense of direction, stability, and peace that makes their lives ultimately more satisfying.

Inviting. Leaders of faith communities want their members to invite others to "come and see" their congregations. Study after study from the past 30 years has shown that the way people become involved in a congregation is not primarily through newspaper advertising, media broadcasts, door-to-door campaigns, or a driving inner desire to belong to a congregation. Rather, by an overwhelming margin, it is through the personal invitation of a friend, family member, or coworker.

In order to measure the inviting factor, we again used a scale of 1 to 5 in asking members of faith communities to respond to the item:

In the last month, I have invited someone to participate in my congregation/parish.

Sixty-four percent of those who were engaged in their congregations said they strongly agreed with this statement. It stands to reason: Those who believe that their congregations are spiritually healthy will feel more positively about them and will naturally want their families and friends to experience the value of being part of them, too. On the other hand, those who do not have positive feelings about their congregations won't be inclined to invite others.

Serving. One of the positive attributes that congregational leaders hope to inspire in their members is a sense of service to others. Members are encouraged to reach out in concern and service to the world, and to help and assist others in their communities and beyond. To measure this sense of service, we asked:

How many volunteer hours a week do you give to help and serve others in your community?

The median number of hours served by those who were engaged in their congregations was 2½, indicating that the spiritual health of a congregation is a significant factor in the serving capacity of its members.

Giving. As is mentioned above, giving is a relevant outcome in determining spiritual health. When compared against the five-year national median household income of $42,300, those who are engaged give more to their congregations than anyone else does — in terms of both percentage of income and actual dollars given. Each year, engaged members give a median of 5% ($2,115) of their annual incomes to their congregations.

OUTCOMES AND CAUSES

In some sense, whether it is intuitively or anecdotally, leaders have known that these outcomes are important to their congregations' spiritual health. And because of this, they have tried to influence these outcomes in hopes of improving their congregations' spiritual health.

The problem is, they've had it backward.

Take, for example, the desire to improve the outcome of inviting. Within Protestantism, there are a variety of "Invite a Friend Sunday" programs. Basically, they all follow about the same pattern. The leadership schedules an Invite a Friend Sunday, and, about six weeks before the event, begins publicizing it to the congregation. The church provides invitation cards for members to give to friends and coworkers; it plasters the building with publicity posters; it gives Sunday school classes lesson plans that deal with the importance of friendship; and the pastor preaches a sermon series on "Friendship in the Bible," all in preparation for the big day. Then, Invite a Friend Sunday arrives, and — if the program has been successful — worship attendance may increase by 25% for that day. But what typically happens in the weeks that follow? Within three or four weeks, attendance is back to its pre-program level. The bump doesn't last.

Let's look at another noble but often misguided effort, this time involving the serving outcome: increasing the number of members who volunteer their time in community outreach projects. Often a congregation will have a "Community Mission Month," with a goal of increasing the number of volunteers the congregation sends to community service projects. Leaders provide information about different organizations, often in the form of a mission fair, in which various community organizations have booths promoting their projects. Again, as with Invite a Friend Sunday, there is a preaching emphasis on service that encourages individuals to volunteer. These efforts produce mediocre results at best — and community service programs in every corner of the nation remain desperate for volunteers.

Once again, the leaders have it backward. They are trying to influence spiritual health by focusing on outcomes. This approach leads to only limited success at best; usually, it leads to frustration and failure.

Outcomes are the result of *causes*. In order to affect the outcomes that are the indicators of spiritual health, leaders must focus on improving the causes of spiritual health. It does not work the other way around.

Gallup research has discovered that the two primary causes of spiritual health are spiritual commitment and congregational engagement. Until now, there has been no way to measure these causes, and thus church and parish leaders have been unable to manage them. And because leaders have had no way of measuring the true causes of spiritual health, they have succumbed to some rather convincing myths about effectively managing their congregations.

It's time to debunk these myths.

DEBUNKING THE MYTHS

Every sector of society has its dominant myths. In business, you often hear, "Our people are our greatest asset," when, in fact, the *right people in the right roles* — not just *anyone in any role* — are a company's greatest asset. Self-help gurus have proclaimed for years, "If you work hard enough, you can achieve anything," when, in reality, you can achieve anything you set your mind to, *as long as you are playing to your greatest talents.*

The truth is, myths can be comfortable. They can even convince us that we are doing the right thing by adhering to them and by planning strategy around them. But wise organizational leaders know when to re-evaluate the myths and let them go in the face of new and persuasive evidence.

Many congregational leaders adhere to three dominant myths when setting priorities and direction for their faith communities. Like most organizational myths, these three are an attempt to describe and make sense of reality. They may even have been useful at one time. But new research has revealed these myths to be false — even detrimental — and it's time to cast them aside in favor of new paradigms.

Myth #1: Believing leads to belonging

According to this myth, an individual's personal spiritual commitment naturally leads to a desire to belong to a faith community. In other words, because someone believes, he or she will also want to belong to a congregation of "like-believers." What's more, adherents to the myth assume that congregational leaders should focus on increasing their members' spiritual commitment, because spiritually committed members will feel a greater sense of belonging and become more engaged in their congregations.

The reality, according to Gallup analysis, is that belonging is far more likely to lead to believing. The extent to which members feel engaged in their faith communities has a profound effect on their personal spiritual commitment. Individuals who are highly engaged in their congregations also tend to have high levels of personal spiritual commitment. The analysis also reveals that congregational leaders who focus their efforts on increasing members' sense of belonging end up not only increasing their members' engagement, but also increasing their spiritual commitment. The more engaged people feel in their congregations, the more spiritually committed they become.

Myth #2: An active member is a faithful member

This myth is rooted in the idea that the members who are the most active in a congregation are also the most loyal. After all, isn't it good to find ways for members to become active? In becoming involved in myriad activities, members get to know each other, they know more about what's going on in the congregation, and they develop an increased sense of ownership — or so the myth goes.

Gallup research has discovered that activity that is not the result of engagement leads to burnout. And burned-out members eventually leave: psychologically, emotionally, spiritually, and physically.

In congregations in which there is activity without engagement — and thus, a high degree of burnout — terms such as "duty" and "responsibility" are repeated in recruiting members for roles. And often the response to such recruiting is, "I've done my share. It's time for the younger members to take their turn."

In contrast, engaged members regularly have the opportunities in their congregations to do what they do best, because leaders have invested the time needed to discover their members' greatest talents and gifts, and have put them in roles they can perform with strength. Such leaders tap into their members' greatest talents and passions — all the while focusing on fulfilling the congregation's mission. These members often don't realize how much service they contribute to their congregations, because they don't think of serving as a duty or responsibility; they most frequently describe it as a joy.

Engaged members do not burn out; they only become stronger, more energized, and more engaged.

Myth #3: Personal faith leads to public action

Acts of service, charity, and goodwill happen as a result of, and in response to, the depth of one's individual spiritual commitment, according to the third myth. After all, as people grow spiritually, don't they naturally desire to reach out in concern and service to the world? And won't they be more likely to invite others to their congregational events — and give more financial support to their congregations?

Individuals who are highly spiritually committed do serve more, invite more, and give more than do individuals who have a low level of spiritual commitment. But Gallup research has revealed that the factor with the greatest influence on these outcomes is engagement. How much members give financially, how many hours they volunteer in community service, and how often they invite others to their congregations are more dependent on engagement than on any other factor.

The message is clear: Leave the old myths behind, and form a new paradigm that's animated by engagement. But first, let's look at the difference between congregational engagement and spiritual commitment.

CHAPTER THREE:
SPIRITUAL COMMITMENT BY THE NUMBERS

Jennifer begins her day early. After she wakes up at 5 a.m., she starts with 30 minutes of prayer, meditation, and Bible reading. She lights a candle on the table by her favorite chair and opens her Bible to the fifth chapter of the Gospel of Mark.

Jennifer is reading through the Bible in a year — and this is the third time she's done it. She is also a member of her church's prayer team; every morning she prays for each person on the prayer request list. When she finishes her prayer time, she extinguishes the candle, works out on her elliptical machine for 30 minutes, hits the shower, and then gets ready for work. By 7:30, she's out the door, headed for her job as a customer service representative for a cable company.

When Jennifer gets to work, she stops by Monica's desk to drop off a "Thinking of you" card. Monica has been going through a rough time — her husband, Tom, was laid off three months ago from his manufacturing job, and her mother was recently diagnosed with cancer. As Monica opens the card, she finds a gift certificate to a local restaurant. "Jennifer, what's this?" she asks.

"Well, you and Tom deserve a break. Go out to dinner Saturday night, and I'll watch the kids for you."

"Jen, I don't know what to say," Monica says, tears coming to her eyes. "You've been such a good friend through all this — listening to all of my problems and knowing just what to say to make me feel better. I don't know what I'd do without a friend like you. Thank you so much!"

"You'd do the same for me, you know. Just keep hanging in there, and I'll keep praying for you and your family. And if you need anything, you be sure to ask, OK?"

Jennifer understands adversity. Jennifer's father died when she was nine, and it was a struggle for her mother to make ends meet — Jennifer is the oldest of five children and was the primary caregiver for her younger siblings while her mother worked at two, and sometimes three, jobs. As a teenager, Jennifer started feeling God's presence within her more and more deeply, giving her strength and guidance, and helping her mature enough to take on heavy responsibilities at such a young age.

She also understands tragedy. When she was 21, her fiancé was killed in a car crash. While he was driving home from his job late one night, a drunk driver crossed the center line and hit him head-on. It took Jennifer a long time to recover emotionally, but looking back she credits living through that nightmare with making her a stronger, more compassionate person. And she says if it weren't for the support of her church, her faith, and God's strong presence in her life, she never would have made it through.

Throughout her work day, Jennifer encounters a multitude of customers, each with their own attitudes: some are angry about mistakes in their bills; some are confused about their service; some are rude when Jennifer can't answer their questions to their liking. But in almost every case, Jennifer is able to make customers feel better about their relationship with the cable company. In fact, she's won several awards for providing outstanding customer service. Jennifer has innate talent for the job, but she also has something else: a strong belief in the goodness of people, a willingness to give them the benefit of the doubt, and a desire to help them solve their problems.

After work, Jennifer meets up with a group of friends at a nearby coffee shop, where she indulges in what she says is her one vice: a turtle latte with extra whipped cream. The friends talk about their work day, laugh with each other, and leave the coffee shop feeling more positive than when they went in.

Later that night as she climbs into bed (after she's called her mother), Jennifer says a prayer of thanks for the blessings of the day, asks God to watch over her friend Monica, and drifts off to sleep thinking about the opportunities that lie ahead tomorrow — like maybe finding out more about the new guy a few desks over from hers . . .

WHAT IS SPIRITUAL COMMITMENT?

Jennifer is the type of person every pastor wants his or her members to become: compassionate, caring, positive, and spiritually committed. But identifying the factors that make up spiritual commitment — and even recognizing the difference between spiritual commitment and congregational engagement — has historically been a daunting and confusing task.

Let's clear up the confusion.

Until now, that difference between spiritual commitment and congregational engagement hasn't been clearly established; many leaders use the terms interchangeably and don't really know how to distinguish them. But spiritual commitment and congregational engagement are distinct concepts with their own unique characteristics. First, let's look at spiritual commitment.

Spiritual commitment reflects a personal depth of spirituality. It is individual in nature, and is seen in both behaviors and attitudes. Our research into spiritual commitment actually began with the work of George Gallup Jr. in the early 1990s. In fact, it was George who first used the phrase "spiritual commitment" to describe a spirituality that went beyond merely an inwardly focused, "feel good" faith to one that made a real difference in daily living.

George devised a 12-item instrument (each item ranked on a 1-to-5 scale) to measure spiritual commitment, and used a relatively straightforward method to determine the different levels of commitment. Those who gave a 4 or 5 to each of the

12 items were spiritually committed, or "saints" (those who gave a 5 to all 12 items were "super-saints"!). George found that, according to his scale, only about 14% of Christians in the United States were saints.

What is most impressive about George's research is his discovery that the spirituality of the saints and super-saints went beyond just a "Jesus and me" self-centered religiosity; it also manifested itself in socially desirable behaviors. The higher the scores respondents gave to the 12 items, the more likely they were to strongly agree with six behaviors, including racial tolerance, forgiveness, and compassion.

In contrast to the image of spiritually committed individuals that is commonly portrayed in the secular media — that beneath their pious exteriors, religious people are mean-spirited, hypocritical, and selfish — George Gallup's research demonstrated that just the opposite was true. The super-saints were far more compassionate, generous, kind, and unselfish than those who were completely spiritually uncommitted — those who gave a "1" to all 12 items.

George was onto something.

His research became the basis for our study of spiritual commitment nearly 10 years later. We added, revised, and analyzed items that measure aspects of individual spiritual commitment, looking for the "differentiating items" — the items that set apart the spiritually committed from everyone else. We wanted the items that the fewest number of individuals could "strongly agree" with; items that would tell us something about the unique nature of spiritual commitment. In the end, we discovered that there were nine items that best measured this pillar of spiritual health:

- My faith is involved in every aspect of my life.

- Because of my faith, I have meaning and purpose in my life.

- My faith gives me an inner peace.

- I am a person who is spiritually committed.

- I spend time in worship or prayer every day.

- Because of my faith, I have forgiven people who have hurt me deeply.

- My faith has called me to develop my given strengths.

- I will take unpopular stands to defend my faith.

- I speak words of kindness to those in need of encouragement.

These items include four attitudes and five behaviors, and when you ask individuals to rank these items on a scale of 1 (strongly disagree) to 5 (strongly agree), you get a pretty accurate picture of a person's spiritual commitment level.

Let's take a closer look at each of the items.

SPIRITUALLY COMMITTED ATTITUDES

My faith is involved in every aspect of my life. Notice the extreme wording here: *every* aspect. It's the use of the word "every" that sets the spiritually committed apart from the rest of the crowd. Spiritually committed people don't compartmentalize their faith or their lives. They don't have their "church box," their "work box," and their "family box"; the stuff of their lives is all in one box. Or, to use another metaphor, the tapestry of their lives is seamlessly woven together, and their faith is the common thread that runs through the entire piece of cloth.

The spiritually committed cannot separate their faith from any other part of their lives, and their faith informs all that they think, say, or do. Their faith has a major impact on all of their decisions. To a large degree, their religious faith influences the way they interact with other people. Their faith permeates their entire being; they cannot imagine existing without a strong spiritual undergirding.

In our research, we have found that 40% of Americans "strongly agree" with this item.

Because of my faith, I have meaning and purpose in my life. This item may seem like a restatement of the first. The difference between the two is that individuals may derive meaning and purpose from their faith without necessarily having that faith involved in every aspect of their lives. In fact, that seems to be the way many people view this item, because more Americans, 55%, strongly agree with this item than strongly agree with the previous one.

It is encouraging that a majority of Americans find meaning and purpose for their lives from their faith. For the spiritually committed, it is not wealth, position, power, or even the pursuit of the American Dream that gives their lives meaning; that meaning is derived from their faith.

My faith gives me an inner peace. The lives of the spiritually committed are not necessarily easier nor do they go more smoothly than the lives of others; in fact, many of the spiritually committed have faced extraordinary hardships in their lives. For some, their spirituality seems to have been forged in the midst of adversity. But through it all, no matter what storms they have weathered in their lives, the spiritually committed find a calm and steady courage. They can face the worst that life dishes out and remain standing, firm in the knowledge that God will see them through. Fifty-eight percent of Americans "strongly agree" with this item.

I am a person who is spiritually committed. This may seem like an obvious statement, but it's not. People who are spiritually committed *know* they are; those who are not committed don't quite understand the item. Fifty percent of Americans strongly agree that they are spiritually committed.

SPIRITUALLY COMMITTED BEHAVIORS

I spend time in worship or prayer every day. There's that extreme wording again: *every* day. The emphasis on "every" day instead of "some" or even "most" days is what makes this a differentiating item, and it sets apart the spiritually committed from the rest of the pack. For the spiritually committed, worship or prayer is just part of their everyday routine; they make room for it, and somehow their day is not complete without their "time with God." Thirty-eight percent of Americans "strongly agree" with this item.

The important thing, however, is *that* they do it, not *how* they do it. For some, like Jennifer at the beginning of this chapter, a time of centering and prayer is how they begin their day. Every morning after the alarm clock rings, their feet hit the floor and they are off to their 30 minutes of prayer and reflection. And these 30 minutes have a definite order to them: 10 minutes of Bible reading, 10 minutes of reading from a devotional book, and 10 minutes of prayer — for self, for the world, and for others. They begin every day this way, and this time alone with God makes them better, more faithful followers of Christ.

For others, their 40-minute commute to work each day becomes a time of prayer and reflection. They put in an inspirational CD and commune with God. On more than one occasion, I've heard individuals refer to their car as their "prayer closet." For still others, their time of prayer and worship comes at the end of the day, as they lay down the cares and burdens of the day, spend time in prayer and Bible reading, and drift off to sleep. Some individuals need this to be "alone time" with God; others meet with a small group on a daily basis at lunch.

The spiritually committed practice daily worship and prayer in a wide variety of ways, depending on what is most meaningful and beneficial for them. But make no mistake: Whatever form it takes, this daily ritual of worship and prayer is vital to their spiritual health and growth.

Because of my faith, I have forgiven people who have hurt me deeply. Forgiveness is a primary tenet of the world's great religions. Christianity, Judaism, Islam, Buddhism, and Hinduism all have doctrines dealing with forgiveness. To be sure, the means and methods of forgiveness differ from religion to religion, but it is definitely an important principle for devotees of these faiths to follow. Inherent in each faith is the recognition that forgiveness without faith is difficult at best, and that faith in something bigger than oneself is necessary. For Christians, forgiveness is at the very heart of faith. They see Jesus' life, death, and resurrection as the primary way individuals are reconciled to God and to each other. Forty-nine percent of Americans strongly agree that their faith gives them the power to forgive.

My faith has called me to develop my given strengths. Only 44% of Americans strongly agree with this statement. What sets the spiritually committed apart is their understanding that they have been uniquely created by God. They believe they have been given unique talents and gifts, and that they have a responsibility to make the most of these talents and gifts in service to God and others.

They realize that their greatest talents and the strengths they have developed truly are gifts from God, not something they have created on their own. As such, they are humble about their talents and strengths; they know that these ultimately are on loan from God. And they also feel God expects them not to just let their talents and strengths go to waste. Rather, they believe they will ultimately be held accountable for the wise use of that with which they have been entrusted. They take seriously the old saying, "Your life is a gift from God. What you do with it is your gift to God."

I will take unpopular stands to defend my faith. Being spiritually committed requires an element of courage; this item measures it. Fifty-four percent of Americans "strongly agree" with this item.

Let's face it: There are many enemies of spiritual commitment. We live in a secular society, and that society suppresses spirituality while promoting the pursuit of material prosperity. But in the midst of this secularism lives a spiritual culture. The innate spirituality of human beings cannot and will not be suppressed; it will always rise to the surface.

Spiritually committed individuals will not compromise their faith, and sometimes must stand firm in the face of secular opposition. This does not mean spiritually committed people are always confrontational; in fact, they are usually just the opposite. They often quietly but noticeably do the difficult and right thing when all others around them are taking the easy way out.

I speak words of kindness to those in need of encouragement. This item measures compassion, a key component of Christian spirituality and of spirituality in other religions. Sixty-one percent of Americans strongly agree with this item, the highest percentage for any of the spiritual commitment items. The reason for this level of agreement may be that the item is the least demanding of the spiritually committed behaviors, or it may be that compassion is a fundamental trait of most human beings. Still, a large enough number of individuals *don't* speak words of kindness to others, and so, the compassion of spiritually committed individuals definitely stands out.

These are the nine items — four attitudes and five behaviors — that are the best indicators of individual spiritual commitment.

THE MISSING PIECE THAT ISN'T REALLY MISSING

As you look at the items, you might be wondering, "Why are there no items about Jesus and the Bible?" This is the counterintuitive answer: Items about Jesus and the Bible actually don't tell us much about spiritual commitment. In our initial study, we asked several "core belief" questions, such as "Jesus Christ is the Son of God," "Jesus Christ was both fully human and fully divine," and "I believe the Bible has authority over what I say and do." We found no significant differences in responses to these items between those who are spiritually committed and those who are not.

Remember the discussion above about "differentiating items"? That's what we were looking for here, as well. While we found that spiritually committed individuals are doctrinally sound, we also discovered that those who are not spiritually committed are nearly as likely to be doctrinally sound. For example, on the "Jesus Christ is the Son of God" item, about 95% of all respondents said they "strongly agree." The item doesn't differentiate; it doesn't separate the spiritually committed from the rest. *Believing all the right things doesn't automatically mean a person is spiritually committed.*

In order to be spiritually committed, you have to go beyond mere belief. Believing the right things — adhering to correct doctrine — is just the beginning. Not only are the spiritually committed doctrinally sound, they go beyond sound doctrine to actually incorporating the tenets of the faith into their daily lives, and then acting on those beliefs — much the way Jennifer, mentioned in the beginning of this chapter, does.

WHO IS FULLY SPIRITUALLY COMMITTED?

According to the latest Gallup data, only one out of seven (14%) Americans are "fully spiritually committed." These rare individuals "strongly agree" with every one of the nine items that measure spiritual commitment. Church membership appears to make a difference in spiritual commitment: 18% of members vs. only 5% of nonmembers are fully spiritually committed.

What's more, members of faith communities outscored nonmembers on *every item* — in many cases doubling or nearly doubling the percentage of "strongly agree" responses from nonmembers. The only item for which the difference is fewer than 19 points is "I speak words of kindness to those in need of encouragement."

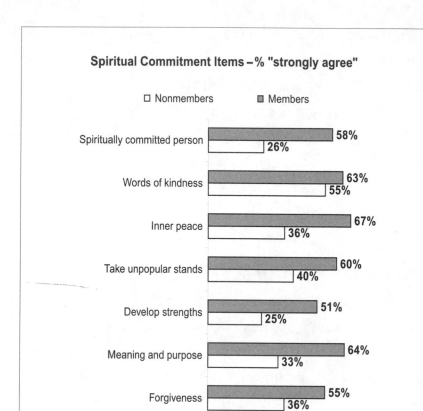

Spiritual Commitment Items –% "strongly agree"

□ Nonmembers ▣ Members

Item	Members	Nonmembers
Spiritually committed person	58%	26%
Words of kindness	63%	55%
Inner peace	67%	36%
Take unpopular stands	60%	40%
Develop strengths	51%	25%
Meaning and purpose	64%	33%
Forgiveness	55%	36%
Faith in every aspect	46%	24%
Worship/Prayer every day	45%	20%

0%   20%   40%   60%   80%

What does a typical fully spiritually committed individual look like? These individuals tend to be older: 41% of the fully spiritually committed are 55 or older, nearly twice the percentage of 18- to 34-year-olds (22%). Spiritual commitment also is higher among women than among men. Seventy-four percent of the fully spiritually committed are women; 26% are men.

African Americans tend to be more spiritually committed than whites are: 19% of blacks are fully spiritually committed, compared with 14% of whites. Full spiritual commitment has a slight downward trend as education increases: 16% of those with high school educations or less are fully spiritually committed, compared with 12% of those with college degrees or more. Widowed individuals tend to be more spiritually committed, as do homemakers and retirees. The prevalence of spiritual commitment also goes down as income goes up: 15% of those with annual household incomes of less than $20,000 are fully spiritually committed, compared with only 9% of those making $75,000 or more.

So if you were to create a profile of a fully spiritually committed person, it would likely be a 67-year-old African-American woman whose husband died within the last year or so. She has a high school diploma, and worked in a service industry job making less than $9 an hour until she retired two years ago on only her Social Security income. To make ends meet, she works part time as a housekeeper at a nearby hotel. At the end of the day, she's tired, she's experienced at least one incident of racial prejudice, her feet hurt and her back aches, and she misses her husband.

But because of her deep faith, she finds the strength to go on living — not just existing, but living: with joy, determination, and a peace that comes from knowing her hope lies not in the things of this world, but in the promises of God in Jesus Christ. She prays and reads the Bible every day, and because of her deep faith, she finds the power to forgive the daily hurts and injustices she experiences. But when needed, she can also summon the resources of her faith and stand up for what's right — without malice or anger.

This woman's experiences definitely do not fit into the "life-styles of the rich and famous." More often than not, spiritual commitment is forged through adversity. Those within whom it is forged truly are the saints among us.

THE FAILURE OF THE PAST 35 YEARS

For at least the past 35 years, the conventional wisdom has been that the decline of the Church in the United States has been because of a lack of spiritual depth among its people. Mainline churches have been particularly susceptible to this criticism; detractors on all sides have been telling mainline churches that they just weren't "spiritual enough" and that they weren't certain enough in their beliefs — these were the reasons for their declining membership.

But during the past 35 years, there has been a huge emphasis on deepening individuals' spiritual lives; witness the multibillion-dollar explosion in the Christian devotional book industry since 1970. Moreover, 41% of American churchgoers participate in small groups for study, support, and service. Add to that the plethora of Bible study and spiritual growth curricula that have been produced by mainline, independent evangelical, and Catholic publishers, and it is hard to imagine a time when there has been more emphasis on individual spiritual growth and commitment than is true today.

Yet with all of the emphasis on increasing individual spiritual commitment that has occurred in the past three and a half decades, only one in seven Americans is fully spiritually committed. One in seven! Something is not working.

It's time to get the order right.

Spiritual commitment is usually a result of one big — and often overlooked — factor: congregational engagement. Focus on improving engagement, and increased commitment will follow.

It's time to prepare the soil. It's time to focus on engagement.

CHAPTER FOUR:
THE ENGAGEMENT IMPERATIVE

It's a typical Wednesday for Mike. After his morning run, he gets ready for work, and then he and his wife, Janet, take their two kids to school.

Over the lunch hour, Mike meets with his men's small group, which gathers weekly to discuss "a Christian approach to men's issues," as Mike puts it. "We started this men's ministry at our church, and I've been involved for about a year now. I can really see a difference in my life."

After work, Mike comes home, works out for an hour, and then the whole family heads out the door for Discovery Night at their church. "There's a meal, activities for the kids, and classes for adults," says Mike. "Janet and I are in a couple's class — made up mostly of people we've invited to our church over the years. Right now we're discovering how our unique God-given talents affect our relationships. It's been great for our marriage."

After their night at church, the family heads home. Mike and Janet check homework, get the children off to bed, watch some TV, and then, before turning in, the couple spends time in prayer together. "It's an important part of our day," says Mike, "to end it together in prayer."

Mike is also involved in leading his church's Habitat for Humanity team. "In my 'day job,' I'm a software engineer," says Mike, "but I've always loved to build things, and even worked construction during the summers I was in college. That's something most people don't know about me. But my church asked me, 'What are you good at, and what do you love to do?' when we became members. I thought about it a while, and I'm also good at organizing people, and I love to build things, and I've really been a believer in the mission of Habitat ever since I saw Jimmy Carter on the news talking about it several years ago. So I talked to the pastor about starting a team from our church. It's been one of the greatest experiences of my life."

For Mike, his faith is the organizing principle of his life. "I wouldn't consider myself a fanatic or anything like that, and I certainly don't press my beliefs on others," he says. "It's just that without my faith, my life wouldn't be as meaningful — I'd be kind of directionless. I don't know how, but it seems that the more I've gotten involved at church, the more spiritually aware I've become. I've become more compassionate, more aware of the suffering of others, and what I can do about it. I'm a better husband and father. I'm just a better person."

WHAT IS CONGREGATIONAL ENGAGEMENT?

Mike is an engaged member of his congregation — and a spiritually committed person.

We need more Mikes in the world. Engaged members, like Mike, drive the spiritual health of every congregation in America. The more engaged members there are in your church, the healthier it is. A spiritually healthy church is the good soil that produces fruit in abundance — and engagement is the key.

Congregational engagement describes the degree of belonging an individual has in his or her congregation. But it is deeper than belonging to a "club"; engaged members use the language of "family" when they talk about their churches. They want to know they are valued and that they make meaningful contributions to the mission and ministry of their churches — not in terms of dollars and cents, but in contributing their greatest talents to accomplish something bigger than themselves.

Through extensive research and analysis, we have discovered that there are essentially three types of members in every congregation: the engaged, the not-engaged, and the actively disengaged. Here's what each type looks like:

Engaged. These members are loyal and have strong psychological and emotional connections to their church or parish. They are more spiritually committed, they are more likely to invite friends, family members, and coworkers to congregational events, and they give more, both financially and in commitment of time. You need to develop more of these individuals, because it is the engaged who drive everything in your church.

Perhaps the key characteristic of engaged members is that their church is top of mind for them. They organize their lives around their church, because it is through it that their faith has grown and deepened; that they have found opportunities to serve and help others in their community; and that they have developed their most meaningful interpersonal relationships. They are proud of their church and they can't imagine a world without it.

Not-Engaged. These members may attend regularly, but they do not have strong psychological or emotional connections to their congregation; their connections are more social than spiritual. They give moderately but not sacrificially, and they may do a minimal amount of volunteering in the community. They are less likely to invite others and more likely to leave.

Two important characteristics are true of the not-engaged. First, they are just as likely as the engaged to be completely "satisfied" with their congregation. Yet the not-engaged give less, serve less, and invite less than the engaged do. That is why responses to "satisfaction" questions are almost meaningless, especially when it comes to congregational life. I can show up at church once a month or so, put $2 in the offering, sleep through the sermon, and actually be "extremely satisfied." But being satisfied doesn't mean I am engaged. Engagement goes beyond just showing up.

The second characteristic to remember is that these not-engaged folks are not negative — they like their church! They are just waiting for an opportunity to become engaged, even though they may not yet know it. As a leader, you should be aware that these folks are your target audience. Find ways to address the engagement issues of these already-receptive individuals and you will improve the overall spiritual health of your congregation.

Actively Disengaged. There are two types of actively disengaged members. The first type usually show up only once or twice a year, if at all. They are on the membership rolls, and can usually tell you what congregation they belong to — but often by location rather than name. I ran into one such actively disengaged member in the first congregation I served after graduating from seminary. I was the associate pastor of one of the largest churches in the community, and during a conversation with a man I met at the grocery store, I mentioned that I was a Methodist minister. He said, "I'm Methodist, too. I go to that big church up on the hill behind the mall."

"Oh, you mean First United Methodist? I'm the associate pastor there," I said.

"Yeah, that's the church!" he replied. "Bill Dorn is the senior pastor there, isn't he?"

"Well, Bill moved 14 years ago," I said.

"Oh, well I don't know the new head guy," the man said — without a hint of embarrassment.

"Actually, the 'new head guy' has been here 14 years," I said, "and he's probably going to be assigned to a new church this spring."

Now, this clueless fellow fits apathetic, active disengagement to a T! And I bet you have folks just like him in your church, too.

However, there is another type of actively disengaged member — one who is quite regular in his or her attendance. These individuals are physically present but psychologically hostile. We call these folks "C.A.V.E. Dwellers": **C**onsistently **A**gainst **V**irtually **E**verything. They are unhappy with their congregation and insist on sharing their misery with just about everyone.

You know who these people are. In fact, if your church has a pictorial directory, you are thumbing through it right now in your mind, picking out the C.A.V.E. Dwellers. You know them by name, you know where they sit on Sunday morning, and you know what committees they are on — and usually dominate.

Their negativity is a huge drain on the effectiveness of your congregation's mission and ministry, and as a leader you probably spend an inordinate amount of time with them. They are the ones who complain, they are the first ones to tell you, "We've never done it that way before," when you come up with an innovative ministry idea, and they are critical of any ministry that does not personally benefit them.

The key to dealing with the C.A.V.E. Dwellers is to *avoid* focusing your energy on them. Rather, focus your efforts on improving engagement, and move people from the not-engaged category into the engaged category. The best chance for the actively disengaged to improve their engagement level is *not* through your attention; it is through their relationships with the not-engaged who are becoming engaged.

This is an important point, and bears emphasizing: *Your job as a leader is not to placate the actively disengaged. It is to create and grow disciples.* And you do that by using strategies that will lead members to become more engaged. In other words, concentrate on creating positive energy in your congregation — enough positivity to neutralize the negativity of the C.A.V.E. Dwellers.

Congregational engagement: The numbers. One reason United States congregations are in trouble is that they have a low percentage of engaged members. Most of the individuals (54%) attending Protestant and Catholic churches are not-engaged, while only 29% are engaged. When you add in the 17% who are actively disengaged, it is little wonder that most local churches are struggling.

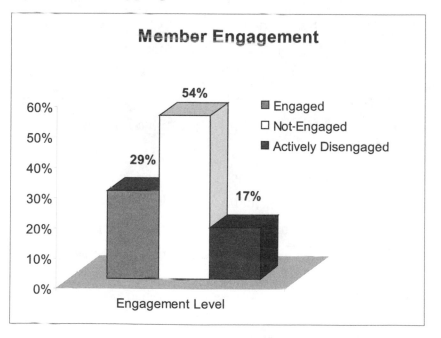

Because we know the actively disengaged are either negative or apathetic, and the not-engaged are satisfied but easily
distracted, it's not a stretch to say that in any given church on
any given Sunday, only 3 out of 10 people really care whether
they are in attendance.

ENGAGEMENT AND SPIRITUAL COMMITMENT

If engagement drives everything, it should have an impact on
spiritual commitment. Indeed, Gallup research confirms that
the two have a powerful relationship. Now remember, only 18%
of American church members are fully spiritually committed
— saying they "strongly agree" with all nine items of spiritual commitment discussed in Chapter Three. But the spiritual
commitment level is *more than twice as high* among engaged
members — 39% of engaged church members are fully spiritually committed. Spiritual commitment drops off precipitously
among not-engaged and actively disengaged members — to
12% and 3%, respectively.

The conventional wisdom is, "believing leads to belonging"
— that is, the deeper one's faith (spiritual commitment) is, the
more likely it is that he or she will desire to belong to a congregation (engagement). The reality is just the opposite: It is
belonging (engagement) that leads to believing (commitment).
So if you want your members to become more spiritually committed, help them become more engaged.

ENGAGEMENT AND OUTCOMES

In Chapter Two, we laid out the four relevant outcomes of a spiritually healthy congregation and noted the effect engagement has on those outcomes. But how do the not-engaged and actively disengaged compare to the engaged on the outcomes? Is there a significant difference setting engaged members apart from the rest? The answer is yes.

Life Satisfaction. Among the general population, only 43% "strongly agree" that they are completely satisfied with their lives — which means nearly 6 out of every 10 Americans are not happy with the way things are going in their lives. That's a lot of unhappiness walking around!

Among those who are engaged in their congregations, however, that ratio is reversed: 61% of the engaged strongly agree that they are completely satisfied with their lives. But as is true for spiritual commitment, life satisfaction falls as engagement declines. Only 40% of not-engaged members "strongly agree" that they are completely satisfied with their lives, and less than one-fourth (23%) of the actively disengaged are completely satisfied. Contrary to the image of "grim Christians" so often portrayed in the popular media, engaged members not only are happier than members who are not-engaged or actively disengaged, they also are happier than the general population.

Inviting. Those who are engaged are *more than 10 times* (64% to 6%) more likely than those who are actively disengaged to strongly agree that they have invited someone to participate in their congregation in the previous month, and are nearly three times more likely than the not-engaged. This is what I meant when I said above that for engaged members, their church is "top of mind." Because they organize their lives around, and have a sense of pride in, their church, inviting others to church events is quite natural for the engaged. But for the vast majority of the not-engaged and actively disengaged, inviting others to come to their church rarely crosses their minds.

It is intriguing that 6% of the actively disengaged actually strongly agree that they've invited someone to church in the last month. I have a hunch a C.A.V.E. Dweller invitation sounds something like this: "Hey, if you think things are bad at your church, you ought to come visit ours sometime; I'll show you a *really* bad church!"

Serving. In the year 2000, according to the leadership forum Independent Sector, roughly 84 million adults aged 21 and older volunteered 15.5 *billion* hours. Look at that number again — this time with zeros: *15,500,000,000 hours!* That's a lot of time spent serving and helping others in the community. Who's doing all this volunteering? According to Gallup research, it's those who are engaged in their congregations.

Engaged members spend a median of 2½ hours per week volunteering in their communities — *in addition to* volunteering within their churches. Those who are not-engaged spend a median of about 1 hour a week, while for the actively disengaged, the median number of hours volunteered per week is 0. That's right: Zero. Nada. Zip. So it appears that a big key to increasing volunteerism in America is for church leaders to focus on increasing the engagement of their membership.

Giving. There's an old story about a pastor who got up before his congregation one Sunday morning and said, "Folks I have some bad news. The city inspector came by a couple of weeks ago, and we have to replace the church roof — and it's going to cost $500,000." A ripple of concern went through the congregation. He continued, "The good news is we already have all the money we need." The ripple of concern turned into an excited buzz. "There's only one problem," the pastor said. "The money is still in your pockets."

This story highlights a significant fact: Churches do not have money; their people do. It is the members who fund the mission and ministry of their churches for the cause of Christ in the world. So who is giving the money? Once again, it is the engaged.

Engaged members give, as a median percentage, 5% (about $2,100) of their annual household incomes to their church. That's nearly twice as much as the not-engaged, who give 3% (about $1,250), and more than three times as much as the actively disengaged, who give 1.5% (about $600). It's another "top of mind" phenomenon: Most families have to think seriously about giving more than $2,000 of their hard-earned income to their church, but it doesn't take much thought at all to put a $10 bill in the collection plate. And remember: These are median figures, which means half give more and half give less.

This is what the relationship between engagement and giving means to your local church: Let's say you have 500 families in your congregation, and they are average in terms of their engagement — 29% engaged, 54% not-engaged, and 17% actively disengaged. The difference between engaged giving and actively disengaged giving is $1,480 per member per year. Because 17% of your members are actively disengaged, that means 85 families are "underperforming" when it comes to their financial stewardship, to the tune of $1,480 each, or an annual shortfall for all actively disengaged families of $125,800. Don't you think that could make a huge difference in accomplishing your church's mission and ministry?

Just wait — it gets more interesting: When you quantify it on a national level, this translates into a nearly *$30 billion* gap between engaged giving and actively disengaged giving.

No doubt about it: Engagement is the primary key to your church's spiritual health. But how do you measure it? How do you prepare the soil, and become a Good Soil church? Before we get to the answers to those questions, I want you to hear Alex's story.

Alex is a native New Yorker. But his experience of New York isn't primarily of skyscrapers and crowded avenues; it's more like that of a small Midwestern city. Although he works in midtown Manhattan, Alex was born, raised, and still lives in Brooklyn Heights. In fact, he is an engaged member of the Episcopal Church where he was confirmed and sang in the choir for 10 years — Grace Church on Hicks Street.

Alex wasn't always engaged, however. He attended services occasionally, and felt that if he was *doing* the work of Christ

— by volunteering at the interfaith homeless shelter, for example — then it didn't matter much whether he went to church on Sundays. However, the arrival of a new rector, Nils, a few years ago changed all of that. "There was something about his leadership that really connected with me," says Alex, "and about the same time he came to Grace, I got married there. I started looking at my life a little differently — maybe a little more deeply — and started going to church much more often."

Alex has maintained that feeling for Grace even since Nils retired, in large part because he connects with the "radically welcoming, open-armed theology" of Nils' successor, Steve. He also finds Steve to be an energizing and inspiring preacher.

About once a month, Alex attends a small prayer group at Grace. And when I say small, I mean *small*: After Alex arrives on a Thursday evening, there are four people in the room: a married couple, Alex, and another man. One particular evening when Alex showed up, there was a sign on the door saying the prayer meeting was canceled that evening. Because it was a warm spring night and Alex's wife was working late, he decided to get some dinner at an outdoor café on Brooklyn Heights' main thoroughfare, Montague Street, and "people watch."

As Alex was relaxing with his meal, the married couple who were part of the prayer group walked by. "Alex!" they said "Steve is preaching at the community Ascension Day service at St. Ann's [a neighboring Episcopal church]; we're on our way over right now. Why don't you join us?" Alex, heartened by the arrival of his prayer partners, readily agreed.

"I wasn't feeling particularly well that evening," recalls Alex, "but something about being invited by this couple who are part of my prayer group really lifted my spirits. And the service itself was just what I needed. I felt a real sense of peace, and physically felt better, too."

After the service, some members of St. Ann's and the couple who were members of Alex's prayer group invited him to stay afterward for a potluck dinner. "I couldn't stay," says Alex, "because I had to get home and see my wife — and pack for a trip the next day.

"But the welcoming atmosphere was just so great. I felt the arms of the Church — not just my church, Grace, but the Church universal — opening up and drawing me in. I felt connected. I felt engaged. This was my Church, and at that moment I was grateful and proud to be part of it."

Alex's experience shows so clearly that engagement is more than involvement. Engagement is about the powerful emotions that connect us to what is most important to us. Good Soil churches recognize those ties that bind, and they open up their arms and draw us in.

The evidence is clear: If you want to grow a spiritually healthy, vibrant, dynamic congregation, focus on increasing the engagement level of your members. In the next chapter, we're going to dive a little deeper and discover what exactly leads to engagement. Here's a hint: It's probably not what you think it is.

Chapter Five:
Measuring Engagement: "What Do I Get?" and "What Do I Give?"

Recently, when I was chopping up some vegetables for dinner, the knife slipped and I cut my finger. Although it wasn't a deep cut, it was enough to send me to the medicine cabinet in search of a Band-Aid. As I was washing the cut and preparing to put on the adhesive strip, I was struck by what an amazing substance blood is, and what you can tell by studying it. At the moment, all I could tell about the blood coming from the cut was that it was red and that I wanted it to stop bleeding. The naked eye didn't reveal much.

But when a medical technician takes a small sample of my blood and uses sophisticated equipment to run tests, it opens a world of information to my doctor during my annual physical. He can determine my cholesterol levels (the good, the bad, and the overall), my thyroid hormone levels, lipids, blood sugar, white cell count, red cell count, and a host of other health indicators — including an indicator for C-reactive protein that, if elevated, can indicate increased risk for heart disease.

That's a tremendous amount of data from such a minute source. But the naked eye is ill-equipped to measure it; it takes special tools and skills to discover the secrets a drop of blood holds.

What's true about blood is also true about churches. By just walking in and looking around a church, or by visiting worship, or even by regularly attending a church for a year, you cannot tell whether it is spiritually healthy — that is, having an optimum level of both spiritual commitment and congregational engagement. A church may display the outward signs that people think are indicative of spiritual health — increased worship attendance and a swelling membership roll — but it may in fact have a serious spiritual illness. It's like the man who runs three miles a day, eats right, and whose is weight is close to ideal — but his cholesterol level is 375. He may *look* like the picture of health, but the blood test reveals the reality that he is a heart attack waiting to happen. Unless you probe beneath the surface and know what to measure, a church, too, can look like the picture of health — but its "blood test" might reveal that all is indeed not well.

So what is the blood test for diagnosing spiritual health? What are the questions that best reveal a congregation's engagement level? Our research team set out to explore these significant problems.

For this groundbreaking work, we studied Christian congregations of all types, both Protestant and Catholic. The vibrant ones had two important characteristics in common: a higher percentage of their members were engaged than was true for the average congregation, and they produced a higher-than-average percentage of spiritually committed individuals. These were Good Soil churches that were producing amazing fruit.

Size and location didn't matter, either. We studied congregations that were small and large; urban and rural; located in the East, the West, the Midwest, and the South; in growing suburban areas and shrinking rural communities. The Good Soil churches, no matter their size and location, all had high percentages of engaged members and high percentages of spiritually committed members. From our research, we discovered 12 items that link most powerfully to the relevant outcomes of life satisfaction, inviting, serving, and giving described in Chapter Two (outcomes that are the best indicators of a church's spiritual health):

1. As a member of my congregation/parish, I know what is expected of me.

2. In my congregation/parish, my spiritual needs are met.

3. In my congregation/parish, I regularly have the opportunity to do what I do best.

4. In the last month, I have received recognition or praise from someone in my congregation/parish.

5. The spiritual leaders in my congregation/parish seem to care about me as a person.

6. There is someone in my congregation/parish who encourages my spiritual development.

7. As a member of my congregation/parish, my opinions seem to count.

8. The mission or purpose of my congregation/parish makes me feel my participation is important.

9. The other members of my congregation/parish are committed to spiritual growth.

10. Aside from family members, I have a best friend in my congregation/parish.

11. In the last six months, someone in my congregation/parish has talked to me about the progress of my spiritual growth.

12. In my congregation/parish, I have opportunities to learn and grow.

The 12 items are intentionally listed in this order. They can be divided into four categories that build upon each other in stages:

1) What do I get?

2) What do I give?

3) Do I belong?

4) How can we grow?

These stages form the following Congregational Engagement Pyramid:

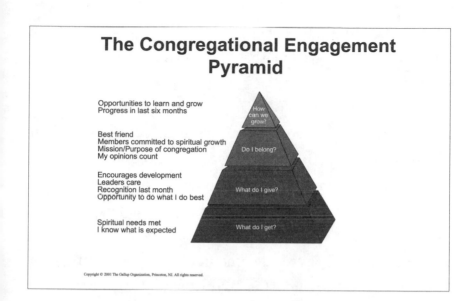

The Congregational Engagement Pyramid

Opportunities to learn and grow
Progress in last six months

How can we grow?

Best friend
Members committed to spiritual growth
Mission/Purpose of congregation
My opinions count

Do I belong?

Encourages development
Leaders care
Recognition last month
Opportunity to do what I do best

What do I give?

Spiritual needs met
I know what is expected

What do I get?

Understanding the stages of the Congregational Engagement Pyramid — and the items that make up each stage — is crucial to improving your congregation's engagement and its overall effectiveness. It is to that end that we now turn our attention to a detailed analysis of the pyramid.

WHAT DO I GET?

The foundation of the pyramid, measured by the first two engagement items, has members asking, "What do I get?" Some have suggested that even asking such a question seems inappropriate because it reflects a rather consumerist attitude toward one's congregation, and that individuals shouldn't focus on what they will receive, but what they can contribute. However, it's a simple fact of human nature that people are more willing to give their time and attention to — and become engaged in — organizations from which they feel they receive something valuable in return. Receiving — spiritually, psychologically, and emotionally — establishes the motivation for giving of oneself.

1. *As a member of my congregation/parish, I know what is expected of me.* How does asking about expectations tap into the question, "What do I get?" Members need to know what is expected of them if they are to develop a strong sense of belonging within their congregation. Clarifying expectations creates a sense of stability, assuring members that they are valued. Being able to answer the question "What do I get?" with "A clear set of expectations" is one of the ways members know they are receiving something of value from their congregation.

Gallup research indicates that 65% of adult congregation or parish members strongly agree that they know what is expected of them. That's a pretty high percentage, and it should be: Knowing what is expected of you, as a member of any organization, is a basic need. Clear expectations are the foundation for engaged church membership.

Although the percentage strongly agreeing with the expectations item is high, a broader look at the data reveals another, more discouraging, dynamic. On a related item, "In the last six months, someone in my congregation/parish has talked to me about the progress of my spiritual growth," only 33% strongly agree. This gap between those who say they know the expectations and those who say someone has talked to them about their progress is significant, because it indicates that there is often little (if any!) follow-up on what is expected of members, and that it is possible for expectations to be *assumed* rather than clarified. As a result, even among the members who say they know the expectations, about half only *think* they know what is expected of them, because in many cases leadership hasn't spelled out or followed up on those expectations.

So the very first thing you, as a leader, must do to ensure congregational effectiveness is to clarify membership expectations. What do you want your members' lives to look like — what is the fruit they should bear as a result of being planted in the soil of your church? What kinds of behaviors are consistent with being a member of your church? Do you want your members to be involved in community service projects? What about frequency of attendance? Should your members be involved in some kind of study, growth, or support group? What do you expect in terms of financial support? These are all questions you can answer by laying out clear membership expectations. Clear expectations lay the foundation for everything else your congregation is called to do and be. Without them, members will drift — eventually, right out the door.

2. *In my congregation/parish, my spiritual needs are met.* This item identifies the characteristic that sets religious communities apart from other charitable organizations: the element of faith. People aren't drawn to congregations or parishes merely because these organizations make a positive impact on the community and the world. Certainly, effective congregations do make positive contributions to their communities, but that is not their primary reason for existence. Congregations and

parishes exist to spiritually transform individual lives. As a result of this transformation, individuals can positively influence their world.

The item, "In my congregation/parish, my spiritual needs are met," is an important one. Indeed, it is the foundation of any congregation's health. So it is a great cause for concern that nationally, only 55% of members strongly agree that their spiritual needs are met in their churches. If members' spiritual needs are not met within their congregations or parishes, they will look elsewhere. Humans are fundamentally spiritual beings, and that spirituality needs to find expression.

Not surprisingly, people who regularly attend worship or Mass are more inclined to say their spiritual needs are met than are those who do not attend regularly. Those whose spiritual needs are met within their congregations have more positive feelings about their membership, and in turn tend to show up at congregational events more often.

However, you must resist the temptation to assume that members' spiritual needs are being met solely through the primary worship service or through attending Mass. While that may be the main source of fulfillment for many members, it is probably not the main source for all members. Other sources may include small groups, Bible classes, support groups, service projects, and mission trips, to name but a few. And even for those who have their needs met by gathering with other members for weekly worship, the reasons may vary significantly. For some, it may be the music, the preaching, the prayers, or the Eucharist. For others, it may be the opportunity to see good friends.

How do you find out what it is about your faith community that meets your members' spiritual needs? Go to them and ask. Hold a series of listening sessions and ask the participants what it is about your congregation that best addresses their needs. The results may surprise you. And then, armed with this information, you can devise strategies to improve and expand upon what your congregation already does well — and thereby reach more people.

WHAT DO I GIVE?

Members must have a clear answer to "What do I get?" in order to become engaged and grow in their faith. Satisfying that need also provides the foundation for the next level of the Congregational Engagement Pyramid, which addresses the question, "What do I give?" A faith community can see how well it is answering this question by looking at survey items three to six.

Human beings have an innate need to give of themselves to help others. Congregations are ideally suited to meet this need, because reaching out in concern and service to others is a primary ethic for most faith communities. Engaged members feel they make a valuable contribution to the effectiveness of their churches — and feel they make a difference in the world.

3. *In my congregation/parish, I regularly have the opportunity to do what I do best.* Gallup research has discovered that

members who regularly have the opportunity to do what they do best within their churches are more engaged than those who don't have this opportunity. But fewer than half of church members (48%) strongly agree that they have such an opportunity.

In the majority of congregations and parishes across the country, individuals' talents and strengths go largely unrecognized — a huge loss of human potential that otherwise could be tapped for the transformation of society. Finding the right fit for people in their congregations — helping them do what they do best — is not just a nice, charitable idea with far-flung, ethereal consequences. It's a practical management objective that is powerfully linked to outcomes that are good for the congregation. Those who strongly agree that they have the opportunity to do what they do best in their churches also volunteer more hours of service in their communities and are far more likely to invite others to participate in their churches.

Overwhelmingly, members who have found the right fit are the best ambassadors for their churches, inviting others to "come and see" while at the same time reaching out in concern and service to their communities and the world. When you help your members discover their greatest talents — and then help them find the right fit to build and apply strengths — you are creating a stronger, healthier congregation.

The notion of focusing on discovering and maximizing natural talents tends to go against the conventional wisdom. In most congregations, there's a perception that there are jobs "anyone can do." Consider the role of greeter. A typical view is,

"Anyone can be a greeter; all you have to do is stand there, shake hands, and make people feel welcome. Besides, it's a great way to meet other members." For those whose talents lead them to naturally think, feel, and behave in ways that make others feel welcome, it really is almost that easy. But for people who are less outgoing and have neither the talent nor the inclination to "schmooze" and make others feel welcome, greeting isn't remotely enjoyable, and trying to perform this role might make them feel like failures — or just plain awkward. I know of one church that tried to institute a greeter program, and it lasted barely a year. Many of the greeters, no doubt quite uncomfortable with the role, didn't even bother to show up!

If, however, you view all jobs and roles as important and meaningful, and therefore insist that they be performed with excellence, and if you understand that everyone has unique talents and strengths, then you can create a culture that values each person's uniqueness and encourages members to maximize their talents in the contributions they make to their church.

Helping members do what they do best is good not only for the congregation, but for individuals as well. Gallup research has shown that individuals have the most room for growth in their areas of greatest talent. Strengths-focused organizations take that concept seriously. Imagine what will happen in your congregation when you unleash that human potential!

4. *In the last month, I have received recognition or praise from someone in my congregation/parish.* Gallup found that only 4 out of 10 members strongly agree with this statement.

Among the 12 congregational engagement items, this one had the second-lowest percentage of "strongly agree" responses.

Leaders often operate by the maxim that "no news is good news" — in other words, they don't offer feedback to their members unless the members are doing something wrong. But Gallup research — and basic psychological and social theory — runs contrary to that approach. Human beings hate to be ignored. We are wired to *need* attention. We thrive on reaction. If we do something we feel is worthy of praise, and consistently hear "no news," we soon give up on that behavior and try something else to get a reaction of some kind. So what are the behaviors you want to see in your members that reflect spiritual maturity? If you can't readily answer that question, take some time to consider it and discuss it with your leaders. Once you've identified the behaviors, reinforce them by recognizing and praising those who display them. But be careful: People can sense "faked" praise. Be generous with praise, but first and foremost be *genuine* with praise.

Recognition should also be appropriate to, and valued by, the individual toward whom it is directed — it isn't "one size fits all." Different people like to be praised or recognized differently. Perhaps you crave public adulation; that doesn't mean everybody does. Not everyone enjoys the Volunteer Appreciation Banquet — some may prefer one-on-one recognition, in the form of a few kind words and a pat on the back. Others may favor a written note, congratulating them on a job well done.

Go beyond treating people as *you* would like to be treated. Instead, treat people as *they* would like to be treated — bearing in mind who they are and what they have accomplished. If you do not know the kind of recognition individuals like, ask them.

Create a "culture of praise" within your church — an environment in which praise is immediate and predictable. Congregations in which praise is frequent will always have a higher level of engagement than do congregations in which praise is rare.

5. *The spiritual leaders in my congregation/parish seem to care about me as a person.* An effective and healthy congregation or parish is one in which people feel safe — safe enough to experiment, to make mistakes, to challenge, to share information, and to support one another. Members of healthy congregations are also better prepared to give their spiritual leaders the benefit of the doubt in decisions about spiritual matters. None of this can happen if individuals don't feel cared about. Relationships are the glue that holds all great churches together. Leaders set the tone, creating a climate in which members feel valued.

In addition, members who feel that their spiritual leaders care about them are far more likely to invite others to take part in their churches. 86% of those who strongly agree that their spiritual leaders care about them also say they have invited someone to participate in their congregation/parish in the last month.

There are no easy steps to follow in relationship building; you cannot force relationships. However, there are some things you can do:

- Be sincere — you can't fake caring.

- Tell people you care — don't assume they know.

- Individualize. Make it a priority to get to know your people.

- Be consistent. Consistency leads to trust, and trust is the foundation of caring.

Your members want to know they are valued, not just for what they can do, but also for who they are individually. When you show an interest in your members' interests and ask about their hopes and dreams, they will feel valued. And feeling valued is an important component of engagement.

6. *There is someone in my congregation/parish who encourages my spiritual development.* This item speaks to the need of congregation members to feel they make a meaningful contribution; 61% of members strongly agree with this statement. If you take an interest in your members and encourage their development, it sends a powerful message. It tells members they have something valuable to contribute, and that others want to help in their development so they can contribute more. When leaders help congregation members grow, it affirms to those members that they are worth the effort.

Similar to the previous item ("The spiritual leaders in my congregation/parish seem to care about me as a person"), this item also appears to be closely linked to the likelihood to invite others to participate in a congregation. Eighty-four percent of those who strongly agree that there is someone in their congregation/parish who encourages their spiritual development also strongly agree that they have invited someone to participate in their congregation/parish in the last month. A possible explanation is that those who are effectively mentored also make the best mentors. Because someone is encouraging these individuals' development, they may be looking for ways to encourage spiritual development in others — and that encouragement may well include inviting others to come and see what is happening in their congregations.

How can you help your members in their spiritual development?

- Challenge your people to deepen their relationship with God — to make spiritual growth a priority. Make belonging to a growth group, Bible study, service/mission group, and the like, part of the expectations of membership.

- Give constant feedback — "hold up the mirror" so that others can see their talents and strengths and find the right fit within the congregation. Spiritual development means helping people discover and obtain what is right for *them*. Most people need assistance with this, and you can do that by helping them reflect on their talents, strengths, and gifts — and whether they are living them out to the fullest in their present roles.

- Be creative in helping people find their callings. Not every person can fulfill his or her calling exclusively through roles within the faith community. In fact, there are far more opportunities to discover one's calling outside the walls of the congregation or parish. You should ask your members three questions when supporting their spiritual development:

  ➢ What are your talents and strengths?

  ➢ What do you love to do?

  ➢ If time and money were no object, what would you do for God?

Creative spiritual leaders will help their members turn their dreams into callings.

Members need to have a positive response to these two questions: "What do I get?" and "What do I give?" in order to begin the process of engagement. They are not the sum total of engagement, but these are the two foundational elements upon which full engagement is built. Once you have established strength in these two areas, you are ready to move on to the final aspects of the engagement process: "Do I belong?" and "How can we grow?"

CHAPTER SIX:
MEASURING ENGAGEMENT: "DO I BELONG?" AND "HOW CAN WE GROW?"

As members decide that they do in fact receive something of value by belonging to their church, and as they discover that they have something to give of themselves that adds value to their congregation, they then start to address the issue of belonging. Their vision becomes less self-focused and more others-focused; as they begin to look at the people around them, they ask whether they really belong with them. The phrase "individual Christian" is an oxymoron; we are meant to live the Christian life in community with others — we are created to belong with and to one another. The third level of the Congregational Engagement Pyramid addresses this issue.

DO I BELONG?

One clear source for a sense of belonging is the congregation's mission statement. The lack of a clearly defined mission can lead to confusion and disillusionment among members.

Consider the experience of a new congregation planted in the suburbs of a mid-sized city. The congregation had been successful in attracting many new members who had not previously belonged to a church. About three years into the church's existence, the leadership went through a process of defining the congregation's mission, vision, and values. The process, which included input from many members, took about four months. The implementation of the mission, vision, and values statement took another eight months, and included a complete reorganization of the congregation's governing structure. But the effort paid off; afterward, the congregation saw a dramatic increase in both attendance and membership. The main contributing factor to this increase, according to the leadership, was that the entire congregation had become quite clear about the specific nature of its mission.

Agreement with the mission gives individuals a clear signal that they fit in with the congregation's culture and have something in common with the other members — in other words, that they do indeed belong.

Here are the items that address the issue of "Do I belong?":

7. *As a member of my congregation/parish, my opinions seem to count.* Our research found that about half (51%) of church members strongly agree with this statement. This low percentage is problematic because churches do not function well when their members feel insignificant or irrelevant. The quickest way for this to happen is for leaders to make decisions that affect

members without first getting their input. Although they may not always agree with their members' opinions, wise leaders will always ask what their members have to say.

Case in point: One congregation was faced with the potentially divisive task of changing worship times to accommodate an additional service in a contemporary style. First, the task force sent information to the congregation, informing members of the need to make changes. It then asked for members' input on the issue, using written surveys, phone interviews, and listening-group sessions. The task force took this information into account, along with regional demographic data, in forming a new schedule.

The next step was to inform the congregation of the new schedule and when it would start, giving members plenty of time to decide which service they would attend. Importantly, members were also given the detailed reasons for the changes. In doing so, the task force acknowledged that a variety of opinions were heard and evaluated. The task force also told the congregation that it would be back in six months with a progress report.

When the six months were up, the task force reported on the progress: worship attendance was up by 33%, Sunday school attendance was up by 42%, and 60% of new members joined as a result of the new service times and format. Even those who did not agree with the changes could see the point of making them, and eventually supported them.

All too often, members feel their opinions are unimportant and not taken seriously by church leadership. Here are a few reasons members may feel their opinions do not count:

- *Their opinions aren't being recognized by the right person.* Sometimes, the primary leader of the congregation is not the best person to receive congregational input. Members may want other people to be paying attention. Perhaps they prefer the lay leadership. Perhaps they want other members to be listening. Finding the right audience for each member is vital. If you do not know who that is, ask.

- *They think the leadership has already made the decision.* Sometimes members say to themselves, "You're asking what I think, but you don't really care. You've already made up your mind." There is a pretty simple solution: Be honest. If you have already made a decision, tell your members that. But if at all possible, involve your members in decisions regarding the congregation. Weigh their ideas, make your decision, and then explain why you made it. Even if some do not agree, honesty will get you a lot further than feigning interest.

- *Your congregation/parish/denomination/diocese has a history of tending to shut people out.* If you're leading a congregation or parish that historically has not cared what its people think, you have a long road ahead of you — but you *can* change the culture. Often, certain channels of communication have become plugged. Ineffective leaders or other individuals may have stifled (or are stifling) the flow of opinions. As a leader, your job is to identify those blocked channels and clear them. If you don't know which communication channels are being blocked (or which individuals are blocking them), ask your members.

Healthy performance on this item boils down to communication, which is vital to the health of any organization — and the larger your congregation is, the more effort it takes to maintain clear lines of communication within it. Finding out what your members think — even if you don't agree with or act on their opinions — is critical to your effectiveness and success.

8. *The mission or purpose of my congregation/parish makes me feel my participation is important.* Congregations and parishes, by their very nature, should be mission-driven. Because of their spiritual underpinnings, churches have more at stake than the financial bottom line or next year's market-share projections. While these are worthy goals for businesses, churches have broader, more eternal goals that address the innate human need to be a part of something bigger than mere existence. That "something bigger" is a sense of mission, and it should affect everything a congregation does. Only a little more than half (56%) strongly agree with this item, and this finding indicates a strong need for congregations to better clarify and communicate their mission to their members.

Every congregation needs a mission statement — something brief, yet comprehensive that concisely sums up why the congregation exists. Many congregations have such statements, but too often, the statements are ineffective because they're too long or unfocused. The mission statement must be short enough to be easily memorized by every congregation member.

Another problem is that many churches create mission statements and then do nothing with them. They're of no use if they're adopted and then forgotten about. Effective congregations organize their governing structure around their mission; measure everything they do by it; educate their current and new members about it; and communicate about it so often that every member has it memorized. For these congregations, the mission represents the guiding force for all they do.

Developing a mission statement is only part of the solution. The challenge is finding a way for each member to connect with the mission. All members, either consciously or subconsciously, ask themselves, "What is the purpose of this church? Is it a purpose I can identify with?" People want to know whether they fit in, and because each member looks at the world in a slightly different way, each comes up with a different answer. One of the key tasks of a congregation's spiritual leaders is to bring the church's mission down to size so individuals can find some connection between the congregation's values and their own.

9. *The other members of my congregation/parish are committed to spiritual growth.* It may sound obvious to say this, but

congregations should be committed to the spiritual growth of their members. If there's no spiritual element in a congregation, how is it different from the Rotary Club or other secular organizations that serve their communities? The connection to "something beyond," the mystical component of congregations, is what sets them apart from other organizations.

Our research found that only 50% of members strongly agree with this item. This could indicate that the members perceive an insufficient emphasis on spiritual growth within their congregations or parishes. Or perhaps members are unsure about what "spiritual growth" really is. Either way, this is a serious cause for concern.

People are not looking for homogeneity in their congregations. The "homogeneous unit principle" — the assertion that people choose to go to churches where everyone else looks, thinks, talks, and acts like them — was a foundational element of the Church Growth Movement of the 1970s, but is out of date in today's world. Americans live in a multicultural society, and they — especially those in their teens, 20s, and 30s — expect their congregations to look like the world they live in. And it's not just cultural diversity that people expect and appreciate, but spiritual diversity as well. While agreement on the central tenets of the faith is crucial, the way in which spirituality is expressed is unique to each individual.

Although members don't expect everyone's spirituality to look the same, they *do* expect a similar commitment to spiritual growth. In addition, members' perceptions of their fellow members' commitment to spiritual growth are a key factor in their likelihood to invite others to the congregation. Sixty-nine percent of congregational members who strongly agree that their fellow members are committed to spiritual growth also strongly agree that they have invited someone to participate in their congregation in the last month.

How do you evaluate the spiritual growth quotient of your congregation? Here are some guidelines:

- *Are your members **expected** to grow spiritually?* It is hard for people to strongly agree with this item if there is no clear expectation of growth — even if that growth is sought after and experienced in different ways. *You* have to make it clear that growth is a priority. What do you expect in terms of personal prayer or meditation? Attendance at congregational events? Small-group or class participation? Service to others? Clarity of expectations will help members make their own commitments, and see commitment in their fellow members.

- *Are your members clear about the mission of your congregation?* This issue was dealt with in greater depth above, but it is highly relevant to this item as well. Spiritual growth should play some part in a church's mission statement. If your members understand that the congregation is mission-driven, then they know that their fellow members are committed to the mission as well.

- *Are you following up on your members' progress?* If members know that someone will be talking to them about the progress of their spiritual growth on a regular basis, they will be far more likely to work on achieving that growth, and to perceive that other members are as committed to spiritual growth as they are.

10. *Aside from family members, I have a best friend in my congregation/parish.* Everyone needs friendships — some more than others, but we are all created as social beings, not meant to live our lives alone. Some psychologists and theologians have claimed that loneliness is the greatest problem of our time, contributing to most of our social ills.

Popular culture has capitalized on our need for relationships, particularly through television. The most popular shows of all time — dramas and comedies alike — are built around relationships among groups of friends. We didn't watch "M*A*S*H" all those years because we were interested in the nuances of the Korean War; we were drawn to the relationships, which were often poignant and downright funny. "Cheers" was built around the relationships developed at a Boston watering hole. The hit show "Friends" dealt with the ups and downs of the relationships of six "twenty-somethings."

There's no getting around it — people need friendships. Yet only 47% of congregation members strongly agree with the statement, "Aside from family members, I have a best friend in my congregation/parish." In fact, only 2 other engagement items of the 12 received lower scores. It seems that deep, meaningful relationships are not being formed in most congregations in this country.

The best congregational environments are those in which there are many real, genuine friendships. Individuals are happiest, most productive, and most fulfilled when they can cooperate and combine their efforts, and when they do not have to waste time watching their backs. Members need to feel they can trust the people around them. Friendship is the gateway to trust; best friendship is proof of trust. Therefore, the more people who feel they can strongly agree with this item, the more genuine trust there is in the congregation and the more effective and healthy the congregation will be.

Here are some strategies for creating an atmosphere in your congregation that encourages members to make deep and lasting friendships:

- *Don't try to make people be friends.* However, you can create the kind of environment in which friendships are encouraged. Remember, relationships are the glue that holds all great congregations and parishes together. As the leader, you set the tone, creating a climate in which members feel valued and relationships are important.

- *Offer opportunities in which there is no agenda except relationship building.* The possibilities are endless: old-fashioned potluck dinners; catered lunches after services; donuts and bagels between services; family outings to the zoo, the beach, parks, and ballgames; dinner groups; cultural events. Use your imagination. And remember: It's OK for congregations to have fun together!

- *Establish small groups.* One of the best ways to encourage deep, lasting friendships is through small-group events. More will be said about this in Chapter Eight.

However you decide to focus on this issue, remember that your congregation is only as strong as the relationships within it.

HOW CAN WE GROW?

This brings us to the question at the top of the Congregational Engagement Pyramid: "How can we grow?" Interestingly, the "opportunities to learn and grow" item received one of the highest percentages of "strongly agree" responses. That would suggest most congregations do a good job of offering classes, workshops, support groups, and other opportunities for spiritual growth. But are the members of these congregations *truly* growing? Additional results show they may not be.

There is a wide discrepancy between the percentage who strongly agree with the "opportunities to learn and grow" item and the percentage who strongly agree with the "progress in the last six months" item. Nearly twice as many people strongly agree with the former (63%) as strongly agree with the latter (33%).

This discrepancy suggests that, while opportunities for growth are abundant, there may not be enough follow-up with members who take advantage of the opportunities. It also indicates that spiritual growth in congregations tends to be self-directed, with little guidance from the spiritual leaders on which opportunities might be most beneficial for each individual. Leaders are not *challenging* their members to grow and helping them find the best ways to do this, but rather are hoping their members will feel challenged to grow on their own. The problem is, many will not. All members need feedback to know how they are progressing spiritually. It is your responsibility to ensure that this is happening for every member of your congregation.

People come to churches expecting to grow; it is up to church leaders to provide opportunities for growth. Beyond providing such opportunities, leaders should follow up and ask members about their experiences in classes, small groups, workshops, and so on. Did they grow? What did they learn as a result of the experience? What difference did participating in the event make in their lives? This not only boosts participant motivation, it gives participants the opportunity to discuss the progress of their spiritual growth, and gives leaders valuable information about the effectiveness of the growth experience.

Here are the items that address the issue of "How can we grow?":

11. *In the last six months, someone in my congregation/parish has talked to me about the progress of my spiritual growth.* Just as members need to know the expectations of church membership,

they also must know how they are progressing in meeting those expectations — particularly in the area of spiritual growth.

Congregations are often woefully inadequate when it comes to providing feedback to members about their progress. In many cases, new members attend a class at which the meaning of membership is discussed, but expectations are seldom clarified. After members complete the class, the only expectations that many congregations even hint at are attendance and financial giving. Members have no way to check their progress regarding spiritual growth because these kinds of expectations have never been clarified. So they go without such criteria, or make up their own — which may or may not be in line with anybody else's. The result: Nobody is on the same page, so it is no wonder many congregations have a hard time defining their mission.

Only one-third of members strongly agree that in the last six months, someone has talked to them about their spiritual growth; this is the lowest "strongly agree" percentage for any of the engagement items. Here are some guidelines to use when developing strategies to improve in this area:

- *How much feedback are your members getting?* All members need feedback to renew their sense of purpose and let them know how far they have come on their spiritual journey. As the spiritual leader of your congregation, it is your job to help them see the signs that they are making progress. With larger congregations, it may not be possible personally to give feedback to every member.

But you can help ensure that the systems and processes are in place so that all members receive regular feedback from someone. Both lay and staff leaders need to be able to give feedback on the progress of those they lead.

• *How can you show your people how far they have come?* There are many techniques for giving feedback. Your leaders will have to find the style that fits them best. However, you can model a feedback process with your staff and key lay leaders, demonstrating a system they can use with members. Here are a few simple methods that everyone can use:

➤ Set up regular meetings to discuss progress. Impromptu feedback is certainly valuable, but the process has more power if it's structured. Ask members how often they would like to meet (once a month, once a quarter, and so on) and then work out a structure that can be followed at each session.

➤ Record each person's successes. Every time you or one of your leaders sees someone doing something or behaving in a way that is particularly praiseworthy, write them a congratulatory note. Obviously, it is also good to congratulate members verbally, but taking time to record your observations in writing carries even more weight.

> Ask your people to track their own learning — and then follow up with them. One of the most powerful ways to encourage your members' growth is to show them how to record the progress of their spiritual journey. Begin by defining "spiritual growth," so members can own the process and check their progress as they grow.

12. *In my congregation/parish, I have opportunities to learn and grow.* As noted above, 63% of members of U.S. congregations strongly agree with this statement. There is an apparent relationship between having opportunities to learn and grow and the likelihood that congregation members will be inclined to reach out and serve their communities. According to Gallup's research, 72% of those who volunteer two or more hours per week in their communities also strongly agree that they have opportunities to learn and grow in their congregations. If you want to encourage more community outreach among your members, provide more opportunities for spiritual growth.

"Opportunities to learn and grow" means different things to different people. Some want to learn from challenging and powerful sermons or homilies. Others prefer short-term classes on subjects that interest them. Some would like to participate in small groups on a long-term basis for support and study. Others favor in-depth Bible studies led by the pastor. Still others want opportunities to serve the poor in their community.

Whether you serve a small congregation or a church of several thousand, a broad variety of opportunities should be presented to meet the needs and desires of your members.

Whose responsibility is it to find and create opportunities for learning and growing? It is your members' — *and* yours. As a spiritual leader, it is part of your job to create the kind of environment in which your members can learn and grow. It is also your responsibility to provide a wide range of learning and growth options. It is your members' responsibility to select from those options, and to track their own growth.

The mere existence of opportunities does not mean everyone is taking advantage of them. Accurate record keeping can help you see whether your members are maximizing the opportunities offered. It is also important to follow up with each of your members on his or her progress. With systems and processes in place to check the progress of members' spiritual growth, you can see how well they are leveraging the learning opportunities offered. You will also begin to see which opportunities seem to be attracting the most people and having the greatest impact. This will help you decide which types of learning and growth opportunities would be most effective within your congregation.

THE BOTTOM LINE

The 12 items are important for one significant reason: More than any other factor, engagement drives a congregation's spiritual health. Only 29% of the members in most U.S.

congregations are engaged, which means over two-thirds aren't really sure why they are there — or whether they want to be there at all.

If members are not engaged, they and the church as a whole don't make any real progress. Members may throw themselves into an activity out of a sense of duty, not because they have a particular passion or strength for the activity or project. These members may be busy, but instead of making progress, they are headed nowhere.

But when members are engaged, they and their congregation move forward. Churches across the country are not making the progress they would like to because they're using less than a third of the human potential available to them. What a tragic waste of time, talent, and energy!

CHAPTER SEVEN:
INSIDE AN ENGAGED CONGREGATION

hat does an engaged congregation look like? What steps does a successfully engaged congregation take to get to an optimum level of engagement? To answer these questions, I'd like to take you inside a church that has successfully worked to become engaged. Now, this isn't a church you're probably visualizing; it's not an independent, fast-growing, high-energy Protestant mega-church in the suburbs of a growing Southern city. This is a Catholic parish in the Northeast — Long Island, to be exact.

I want to introduce you to St. Gerard Majella Catholic Church in Port Jefferson Station, New York. It's a parish that has about 4,000 families within its boundaries and about 1,200 active families, and it partners with three other parishes in a regional Catholic school. On the surface, you would find nothing remarkable about St. Gerard. But if you did a "blood test" of the parish, you'd discover an exciting, vibrant, and growing community of committed Christian disciples.

I chose St. Gerard Majella in order to show that engagement does not depend on location, worship style, tradition, or ecclesiology. Rather, it depends on applying the principles described in this book. And any leader, if he or she is willing to do the work involved, can improve the engagement level — and subsequently the spiritual health — of his or her congregation.

But it does take work and persistence. Engagement does not happen overnight, and there is no magic pill you can give each of your members to make them more engaged. However, if you stick to it and apply what you've learned, and incorporate strategies to address the 12 items that measure engagement, you will succeed in improving the soil of your church — and become a Good Soil church that produces amazing fruit.

THE BEGINNING: A FOCUS ON OUTCOMES

The story of St. Gerard Majella's journey toward engagement really began in 1991, when Father Bill Hanson and Father Chris Heller were appointed co-pastors to this rather nondescript parish in a middle-class neighborhood of Long Island. St. Gerard wasn't the biggest parish in the diocese, and it was far from the most prestigious. The building was constructed as multi-use space and didn't include a permanent sanctuary. It was tucked away in the neighborhood, on a side street with no distinguishing landmarks. In other words, you had to be intentional about getting to St. Gerard, because it wasn't really "on the way" to anywhere else.

Frs. Bill and Chris came to a parish that didn't have a clear understanding of why it existed. OK, if you were Catholic and lived inside its boundaries, you were supposed to go there, but there wasn't much to draw you in. Most of the congregants had a nonchalant attitude about their church: they knew it was there, they went when they had to, and didn't let church "interfere" with their real lives.

St. Gerard also had a $500,000 debt.

But Fr. Bill and Fr. Chris were men of commitment, passion, and vision. They also loved people and were determined to turn St. Gerard around. They knew they had to give St. Gerard a sense of purpose, and so they adopted a mission statement for the parish based on Acts 2:42-46:

> *They devoted themselves to the Apostles' instruction (Evangelization), and the Common Life (Community), the Breaking of the Bread, and the Prayers (Liturgy). A reverent fear overcame them all, for many wonders and signs were performed by the Apostles. Those who believed shared all things in common; they would sell their property and goods, dividing everything on the basis of each one's need (Service).*

The two priests then created a visual metaphor around the four elements of their mission statement.

SERVICE / HARVESTING
...We help each other...

EVANGELIZATION / SEEDING
...We inspire each other...

LITURGY / POLLINATING
...We pray with each other...

COMMUNITY / TENDING
...We enjoy each other...

They were spurred on in their efforts by the release of the Bishops' Pastoral Letter on Stewardship, which had as one of its central themes that "Once one chooses to become a disciple of Jesus Christ, stewardship is not an option" — stewardship of treasure, stewardship of vocation, stewardship of the Church; in short, stewardship of all of life. Fr. Bill and Fr. Chris believed that their mission statement for St. Gerard Majella addressed the major themes of the Pastoral Letter.

They also believed in creating a climate of financial stewardship, so they implemented an expectation of proportional giving among their parishioners. They advocated a "take a step" approach to stewardship, encouraging members to "step up" to tithing in 1% increments. Slowly but surely, the situation at St. Gerard began to turn around. A symbol of the change that was occurring was the transformation of the parish gift shop. What was once an actual shop selling rosary beads and other items became an office space for a parish "gifts coordinator," who helped connect members to ministry opportunities based on their talents and gifts.

THE ENGAGEMENT CONNECTION

Analytical and always pushing forward, Fr. Bill and Fr. Chris asked questions about their parish — questions that leaders who want their churches to grow often ask:

- Why don't more people join our church?

- Why don't they stay?

- Why don't they serve?

These questions were constantly on their minds, and they kept searching for the answers. Then it dawned on them: Maybe they were asking the wrong questions! Maybe they should turn them upside down, and instead look at them from a positive point of view:

- Why *do* people join our church?
- Why *do* they stay?
- Why *do* they serve?

They were convinced that the answers to these questions would tell them more about St. Gerard and its strengths and potential than would their negative counterparts. But how would they go about measuring responses to these questions? And how would they relate them to their mission of inviting, serving, giving, and thanking? These were questions they wrestled with continuously.

About the time that Fr. Bill and Fr. Chris decided to start asking different questions to find out more about their parish, they became aware of the research our team at Gallup was doing in congregational engagement. They soon realized, much to their delight, that the four relevant outcomes we identified as inviting, serving, giving, and life satisfaction were almost identical to their mission statement. And it was even more exciting to them that we had identified the items that influence the outcomes.

They decided to ask us to help them measure engagement in their parish, and four years ago, as of this writing, they began using our tools to help them measure and improve it.

Over a four-year period, St. Gerard has measured engagement six times, and Fr. Bill, Fr. Chris, and the lay leadership have implemented strategies to increase the proportion of engaged members in their parish. They have incorporated the taxonomy of engagement into parish life, so that members know the difference between engaged, not-engaged, and actively disengaged members. Members have made banners that ring their worship center, depicting each of the 12 engagement items so all parishioners can see what engagement means — and what is expected of them in response.

They have clarified the expectations of membership — and revisit those expectations on a regular basis. They have expanded the "take a step" approach beyond financial stewardship to include the outcomes of engagement, urging members to take a step forward in serving, in learning and growing, and in inviting. They have used the imagery of the blood test to get their members used to the idea of and the importance of measurement to determine the health of their parish.

They have seen engagement grow during this four-year period, from 34% engaged to 46% engaged.

What's more impressive, however, is that St. Gerard has cut the percentage of actively disengaged members by *nearly half* — from 22% to 12%. And the parish accomplished this decrease by *not focusing on it!* Instead, members and leaders emphasized the positive, and devoted their efforts to increasing engagement. As a result, active disengagement went down without the parish's dedicating an inordinate amount of time and resources to addressing it.

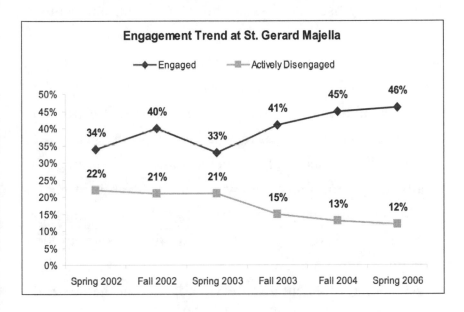

Now, the members of St. Gerard Majella are no longer nonchalant about their faith. Walk into any event at St. Gerard, and you'll find a palpable sense of excitement and positivity. God's Holy Spirit is moving at St. Gerard in a way that's truly remarkable; some would call it a miracle. But it's a miracle that took vision, perseverance, and a lot of hard work to bring about.

Oh yes — remember that $500,000 debt? It's now a $2 million surplus, part of a campaign to construct a new church building.

THE POWER OF THE RIGHT FIT

One of the most powerful strategies Fr. Bill and Fr. Chris implemented during their measurement of engagement was helping people discover what they do best. They decided to use the Clifton StrengthsFinder — an online assessment that identifies an individual's five "Signature Themes" of talent — in their small church groups as an exercise in self-discovery and spiritual growth. (The themes are drawn from a taxonomy of 34. Examples of themes include Achiever, Learner, Relator, and Strategic.) That turned out to be the decision that really took things to the next level: The excitement and enthusiasm of the small-church group members who were involved in strengths development spilled over into the rest of the parish, and now members call in to the parish office wanting to sign up for a strengths group.

At St. Gerard, talent discovery is not just another program, but is an integral part of the fabric of the parish — the language of talent and the Clifton StrengthsFinder are a basic part of its culture. As you walk into St. Gerard, one of the first things you notice in the lobby/narthex area is what the parish calls its "Wall of Fame." All members who have received a Clifton StrengthsFinder assessment have their pictures posted on the wall, and beneath each picture, the person's five Signature Themes of talent are listed. Staff members — both clergy and lay — have shirts with their Signature Themes embroidered on them. Fr. Bill is frequently seen in a polo shirt that lists his top five themes: Connectedness, Ideation, Learner, Self-Assurance, and Responsibility.

Every member who has received a Clifton StrengthsFinder assessment also has a lanyard-style name tag with his or her picture and Signature Themes on it. Lifting up the unique talents of individuals helps others recognize the extraordinary way in which we all are created, and celebrates the special contribution each person can make to the community and to the mission of the Church.

It doesn't stop there. Marie Guido, the gifts coordinator whose office used to be in the now-defunct gift shop, sees the unique way God creates people as a powerful way for them to discover avenues for ministry. She has countless stories of transformation to tell about people who have discovered their greatest talents and then have identified for themselves a ministry that fits their talents. "It is so amazing," Marie says, "to see people discover their strengths and then *they* see a ministry that is right for them — instead of us having to go out recruiting to 'fill slots'! It is so refreshing and such a joy!"

THE FRUITS OF ENGAGEMENT

Focusing on engagement has given the leadership of St. Gerard a new freedom. Instead of just trying to guess what programs and strategies will address issues and needs in the church, leaders can concentrate their efforts on what will really make a difference in how their church functions. They have also been able to address concerns with accurate information rather than speculation.

Accurate information also comes in handy when addressing objections of the actively disengaged. Fr. Bill was approached once by a woman who said, "I don't think I like all the changes that are going on here and all this measurement stuff — and there are a lot of other people I've talked to who feel the same way!"

Fr. Bill replied, "I understand your concerns, but you should know that 13% of the congregation agrees with you, and 45% agree with the direction we're going." The woman was speechless. She has since decided that the direction of the congregation really is for the best, and has started to become more engaged.

"As I look back on the incident," recalls Fr. Bill, "I was amazed at how calm I was in responding. Usually a comment like that would tear me apart, and I'd be saying to myself, 'What if it's true? What if there really are a lot of people who don't like where we're going?' And I'd be filled with self-doubt. But now that I know what the numbers are, I have accurate information that *really* tells me how we're doing."

NAVIGATING A BIG CHANGE

About two years into their measurement of engagement, the Bishop informed Fr. Bill and Fr. Chris that, because of the shortage of priests, Fr. Chris was going to be moved to a parish on the other side of the diocese. The two priests informed the members of St. Gerard, who were understandably saddened by the news. Fr. Chris was beloved by the church, and his leadership had been greatly appreciated.

But what's fascinating and totally counterintuitive — and an indication of the power of engagement — is that when the church did its engagement measurement a few months after the announcement, the percentage of engaged members actually *increased*. That is not typical; engagement usually *decreases* when there is a change in leadership.

"I attribute it to the spirit of our members," says Fr. Bill. "In conversation after conversation, people would tell me that they would have to become more involved in the church because Chris was leaving. They knew his departure would leave a void, and they would have to step up to fill it. They also knew they would have to step up and do more because we would be down to one priest, and they didn't want to lose the momentum we had going. I'm so proud of them!"

I hope you get a sense from this case study of what an engaged congregation looks and feels like. Your congregation can be like this, too. You can improve your congregation's engagement level, and not just "do church" anymore, but experience the joy of truly *being* the Church. In the next chapter, I'll share some strategies on how you can get started.

Chapter Eight:
Strategies for Improving Engagement

At this point you may be saying to yourself, "This is really eye-opening information. But what am I supposed to do with it? How can I start putting into practice all this new knowledge? What should I do first?" This chapter will help you begin to answer those questions, and will offer some practical strategies that you can start implementing right away.

Beware of trying to do too much too fast — don't try to work on improving all the areas of engagement at once. The comic Stephen Wright says, "You can't have everything; where would you put it?" Likewise, you can't *do* everything, either. When would you do it?

So if you were to ask me what three things you should work on that would have the greatest immediate impact on your church's engagement, I would say these:

- clarify the expectations of membership
- help your members discover what they do best
- create small groups

Start with these, and you'll be well on your way to improving your church's spiritual health. You'll also begin to see improvement in the outcomes described in Chapter Two: life satisfaction, inviting, serving, and giving.

CLARIFY THE EXPECTATIONS OF MEMBERSHIP

It was a sad day in my life when Bill Watterson decided to retire from drawing his brilliant comic strip, "Calvin and Hobbes." The strip featured Calvin, a six-year-old boy, and his "stuffed" tiger, Hobbes — who appeared as a real tiger when alone with Calvin, but was just a toy when in the presence of others. Calvin and Hobbes had many adventures together that included haircuts, inventions made from a cardboard box, a time-traveling red wagon, and tormenting the babysitter — much to the bewilderment of Calvin's parents.

Calvin and Hobbes played a fantastic game called "Calvinball," which included masks, balls, flags, and rules that could be changed by any player at any time. The only permanent rule of Calvinball was that "You can't play it the same way twice."

A good number of church members are playing their own version of Calvinball, and they don't even know it.

Most denominations (and congregations!) operate much like this: Adolescents go through the confirmation/baptism/consecration process in a class that lasts anywhere from six weeks to two years; they learn what it means to be a member of their particular church (the expectations); and they are confirmed/baptized/consecrated as members. They are then expected to remember the expectations of membership for the next 60 years, because this is the last time these expectations will be clarified for them!

Members transfer their membership from one church to another, perhaps attending an afternoon welcome class, but never are the expectations of membership revisited; after all, "They went through all that in confirmation."

I'm one of those people who can't remember where I put the car keys when I came home from work an hour ago and who can't recall more than three things I'm supposed to get at the grocery store without making a list. And yet I'm supposed to remember expectations of church membership that I learned 35 years ago when I was 12 years old — and had a whole lot on my mind other than paying attention in confirmation class?

I can't stress it enough: People need to know what is expected of them as members of their church; they need to know "the rules of the game." Otherwise, they will make up their own rules — just like a game of Calvinball. And those rules may or may not be in line with what *you* expect from church members.

It's time to get real, folks. We as church leaders have done a pretty miserable job of clarifying and reinforcing the expectations of membership in our churches. Our members need the security that comes from knowing the rules of the game so that they can have the confidence and assurance to step out and take risks in their faith. If they don't know what's expected, how can they grow in their faith?

Expectations are a two-way street, though. Not only do people need to know what is expected *of them*, they also need to know what to expect *from their church*. What can they expect in terms of assistance with their spiritual growth, opportunities to learn, support in difficult times? Again, this provides a sense of assurance. But it also creates a mutual accountability: Individuals know where they stand, what they can expect from each other, and what they can expect from their congregation or parish.

This may sound adversarial, but it's not. The best, most satisfying interpersonal relationships have this kind of reciprocity regarding expectations. In relationships of trust, respect, and caring, both parties know what they can expect from one another — and fulfilling and exceeding the expectations of the other can be genuinely satisfying. Knowing where we stand with each other also sets us free to risk, to be vulnerable, to grow. Church membership should be no less fulfilling.

Here's how I addressed the issue of expectations as a founding pastor of a new church I helped plant in the 1990s. We put together a Covenant of Membership, which laid out what was expected from members — and what they could expect from their church. Now, we didn't raise the bar particularly high (the church was United Methodist, after all, and there were valid theological and ecclesial reasons for minimal membership requirements), but it was more than most churches in our tribe were doing at the time.

The covenant was printed on a single sheet of paper with two columns. On one side of the covenant were the expectations of membership, which were basically an expansion of the traditional United Methodist membership vows to support the church with our prayers, presence, gifts, and service:

As a member of St. Andrew's, I will:

- support and further the mission of St. Andrew's: to share the Gospel of Jesus Christ

- pray for my church and fellow members regularly

- be present in worship and other church events on a regular basis

- support my church with my spiritual and financial gifts

- find an area of ministry through which I can serve Christ and others

We then left space for them to sign and date this side of the covenant.

In the other column, we listed what the members could expect from us. This side of the covenant mirrored the vision statement that we created to support our mission:

As your church family, we will:

- provide opportunities for you to live out your faith in service to others

- provide faith-building opportunities for you to grow as a Christian

- provide opportunities for you to develop deep and lasting friendships in community with others

- provide opportunities for lifelong learning as you deepen your understanding of the Bible and the Christian faith

- be good stewards of your financial contributions to your church

At the bottom of this column were two spaces for the lay leader's and my signatures.

That's all there was to it; as I said above, we didn't raise the bar particularly high. But it was interesting to see people's reactions when we asked all our members to sign it — both existing members and new ones. We implemented the covenant four years into our existence, and so we had hundreds of members for whom a covenant was a new and puzzling thing, and they weren't so sure they liked it. The strongest negative reaction came from members who had "been Methodist all their lives" and had never had to sign a covenant before — why now?

We explained that we took church membership seriously, that people could make choices, and they could choose to join, or not join, a church. We wanted to honor that choice with a covenant, which we would renew every year on the anniversary of our church's founding — Charter Sunday. We also explained that this would put everyone, new and current members, on the same page. There was some grumbling, but most of the current members signed the covenant.

On Charter Sunday, we had a celebration of our founding, with special music from our band, and singers, balloons, special guest appearances — and a service of "Covenant Renewal." During the time of Covenant Renewal, we had members come forward and place their signed covenants in a basket on the Communion Table, where I then said a prayer of dedication over them. It was a symbolic and touching moment, and I think all of us knew how important that Covenant Renewal was. Each year on Charter Sunday from then on until I moved to another church, we all renewed our Covenant of Membership. And there were no more negative comments or questions — we all understood the importance of the covenant.

That is just one way to reinforce the expectations. You can probably think of several other, more effective ways to do it. One church I know organizes its annual report around its membership expectations, and then reports its measurements of how well the congregation did in meeting those expectations. The important thing is to clarify and reinforce the expectations of membership. You will see an increase in your members' engagement as a result.

HELP YOUR MEMBERS DISCOVER WHAT THEY DO BEST

People are most likely to be fully engaged when they are doing what they do best. When they are asked to do something they do not have much talent for or interest in, they tend to go through the motions without feeling like they're making a significant contribution. People who get to do what they do best in their congregations — or whose congregations help them discover what they do best — have a deep sense of being appreciated for their specific contributions. They are more likely to be engaged than actively disengaged.

Our research bears this out. We compared the engagement levels of three congregations, paying particular attention to those in each congregation who strongly agreed that they have the opportunity to do what they do best in their congregation. The results were striking: Members who strongly agreed that they have the opportunity to do what they do best were *more than 2½ times as likely* as the average member to be engaged (76% to 29%), and *38 times as likely* to be engaged as they were to be actively disengaged (76% to 2%). In fact, active disengagement among these groups in each church was between 1% and 2%, which is statistically insignificant: in lay terms, it's just about zero.

Engaged members give their best to their church, and they are at their best when they do what they naturally do best. Unfortunately, as I discussed earlier in the book, the conventional wisdom is that new members become loyal merely by being active. So give them a job to do, and any job will do. Most of the time, leaders start with the role, and then find a person to fill it — instead of starting with the person and then creating a role to fit the person. This leads to all kinds of problems.

Many churches have a nominating committee charged with filling vacancies on church boards and committees. The nominating committee meets a few times a year, usually before the church's annual meeting, and considers all the "slots" it has to fill. Then committee members start going through the membership list and the pictorial directory to find enough people to fill these slots. The goal is to have a full slate of nominees, rather than to help individuals find a ministry that fits their talents and gifts.

Then, almost invariably, and with the best of intentions, someone comes across "Tom and Cheryl Smith," who used to be active but now are rarely in church. Instead of going to Tom and Cheryl and asking them why this is, the committee typically comes up with a different solution. "You know what we should do," says a well-meaning member of the nominating committee. "We should put them on the church council. That way, Tom and Cheryl will know what's going on and they'll start coming to church again." Now I don't know about you, but I've met few people who were inspired to start coming more often to worship services or Mass by attending church committee meetings.

So Tom and Cheryl are called to serve on the church council, and they reluctantly do so — because they feel guilty about becoming lax in their church attendance. They used to attend when their children were active in the youth choir — even serving as youth sponsors and as members of the Youth Advisory Council. But now that their youngest is in college and they no longer have kids involved in the youth program . . . well, they've just sort of drifted away.

When they receive their postcard in the mail, informing them of the next church council meeting, Tom and Cheryl show up — along with the other 125 members of the council — and dutifully sit through two hours of report after report after report, each one followed by a vote of the council to accept the report. The only excitement comes when a proposal to paint the nursery (that first came to the council six months ago) is discussed (again) and referred (again), this time to the children's ministry committee. It is the first and last church council meeting Tom and Cheryl attend, and they stop coming to church altogether, becoming actively disengaged through neglect.

People like Tom and Cheryl exist in every congregation. They once were involved (but not really engaged), but because they were not doing what they naturally do best — instead, they were filling slots on committees — they became burned out. And burned-out members eventually leave. They leave psychologically: Their church is no longer top of mind for them. They leave emotionally: They just don't have the same passion they once had for their congregation or parish. They leave spiritually: One of the comments you'll hear the burned-out make is they just don't feel like they are being "fed" at their church anymore.

And then they leave physically. In a best-case scenario, Tom and Cheryl's pastor gets a call from a church across town, asking for a transfer of their membership. But it's more likely that Tom and Cheryl will find something else to do on their weekends, and other organizations in which to invest their talents, and they are eventually removed from the church rolls. And, other than attending an occasional Christmas Eve service, they never set foot in a church again.

Engaged members, however, do what they do best — and often don't realize how much they do. They don't *only* do what they do best; but because they serve in areas that make the most of their talents, they have the energy and desire to pitch in and help in areas where they are *not* particularly talented. Says one engaged member, whose main area of service matches her talents perfectly: "I never realized how much I do here until I sat down and counted it up one time. It doesn't feel like a burden; instead, it's a joy to serve." Members who serve in a role they love and for which they are especially talented only get stronger, more energized, and more engaged.

How do you connect people to ministries for which they are particularly suited? You begin with the person and then find or create the ministry. Start by asking three questions:

1. What are your talents and strengths?

2. What do you love to do?

3. If time and money were no object, what would you do for God?

The answers to these questions will help you begin to discover your members' talents and strengths, and then develop ministry opportunities around them.

But if you're really serious about taking a talent-based approach to ministry, I would urge you to read *Living Your*

Strengths, the book I co-authored with Don Clifton and Curt Liesveld, and explore in-depth the possibilities for ministry that occur when individuals focus on developing their greatest talents. *Living Your Strengths* also includes one Clifton StrengthsFinder assessment. There is so much you can do to help your members do what they do best — more than I can include in this book — and I strongly believe in the power of the right fit to drive the engagement of your members. *Living Your Strengths*, and the companion small-group study, *The Living Your Strengths Journey*, will help you accomplish that.

CREATE SMALL GROUPS

For many of you, the importance of small groups is not a new concept. In fact, some of you have been leaders in the small-group movement, which has grown significantly in American culture for the past two decades, not just in congregations but also in other areas of life. In fact, our research finds that 41% of American church members belong to a small group. Princeton Sociologist Robert Wuthnow calls this phenomenon "the quiet revolution," and church members involved in it are more engaged than those who aren't involved — by a wide margin.

If your church is already participating in the "revolution," you are no doubt experiencing the benefits that small groups bring, not only to the individual lives of your members, but also in the overall life of your church. Forty-three percent of those who belong to a small group are engaged — more than double the percentage of those who do not belong (18%). And small-group members are much less likely to be actively disengaged than those who aren't part of a small group: 9% vs. 24%, respectively. What's more, those who belong to a small group score significantly higher on every item of engagement — an average of 18 points higher! Take a look at the following chart — the difference is striking:

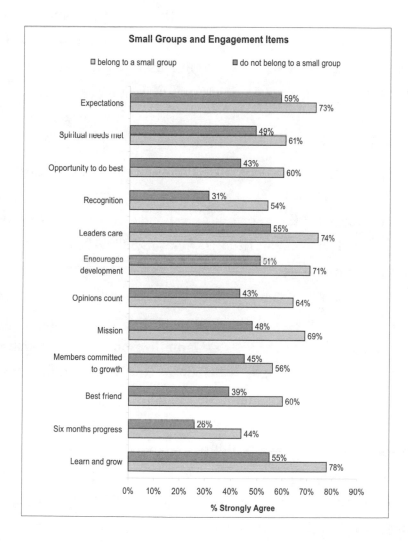

Does being engaged move members to join small groups? Or does being a member of a small group create a stronger sense of engagement in one's congregation or parish? That's a chicken-or-egg question. It well may be that engaged members, seeking to deepen their spiritual commitment, decide to join a small group. As noted church consultant Bill Easum has observed, conversion may happen through the primary worship service — but discipleship happens in small groups. So it's fairly easy to see how a growing sense of engagement could lead members to join small groups in order to further learn and grow.

But it's also easy to see how belonging to a small group increases one's engagement. Among other things, small groups offer opportunities for members to form deep and lasting friendships, have their spiritual needs met, learn and grow, be encouraged in their spiritual development, feel cared about, and see spiritual growth in others. So it's not an "either/or"; it's a "both/and" when it comes to small groups and congregational engagement. What is important is there's a significant relationship between the two. Capitalize on this relationship — no matter which leads to which — and your congregation will become much healthier.

There is great potential for starting numerous small groups in your church. Some possibilities include:

Study groups. These groups meet to study Scripture, books, video series, or a variety of other subjects. Their purpose is for participants to learn and grow.

Talent discovery and strengths development groups. The experience of St. Gerard Majella Church in the previous chapter shows that groups that focus on identifying members' talents create a tremendous bond among those members. As members encourage one another in developing those talents into strengths, the spiritual journey they take together deepens their faith.

Accountability groups. These groups meet in order to help participants face the challenges of everyday life and become better people. Members hold each other accountable for living up to the expectations of their faith tradition, and encourage each other in their efforts.

Support groups. These address myriad problems people deal with in their lives, and offer the assistance and encouragement of others who are facing or who have faced similar difficulties. Support groups may be centered around divorce recovery, depression, grief, living with cancer or other diseases, addictions, parenting teenagers, and so forth.

If you stop and think about it, Jesus did most of his ministry in small groups. Although it was his public ministry — teaching, healing, miracle-working — that brought him notoriety in first-century Palestine, it was through his small group of 12 disciples that he really left his legacy and changed the world. Jesus spent time with them sharing teachings he never revealed to the public, explaining the Scriptures to them, trying to help them understand exactly what God intended for them. After his death and resurrection, the 11 remaining members of Jesus' small group stuck together (primarily out of fear and confusion) until the Holy Spirit revealed to them how they were to go about proclaiming the Gospel — and changing the world.

Being part of a small group profoundly changed the lives of those disciples. That kind of powerful transformation still happens today — usually not as dramatically, but just as profoundly. Give the members of your church that kind of opportunity; help them be part of a small group.

Chapter Nine:
The Dynamics of Engagement

One of the most powerful things we've learned about engagement is that it's not static, but dynamic and fluid. Engagement is also organic; it grows and shrinks, breathes in and breathes out in response to conditions within a congregation, and in response to external influences on a congregation.

There are also similarities between congregational engagement levels and workplace engagement levels. In fact, the quest to discover the determining factors of congregational engagement has its roots in Gallup's research on workplace engagement. Gallup discovered that engagement drives business outcomes. Outcomes of productivity, profitability, customer engagement, turnover, safety, and absenteeism are all dramatically influenced by the engagement level of employees.

Researchers also found that engagement drives outcomes, no matter what the business or where it's located. Engagement is the same, whether it be in the hotel industry, banking, retail stores, sales organizations, manufacturing industries, even hospitals and schools. And the measures of engagement are the same, no matter the country or culture — whether the organization is in Chicago, or Mexico City, London, Mumbai, Singapore, or Budapest. Engagement measures what's important to individuals about belonging to their organizations. In any organization — workplace or not — people need to answer these questions:

- What do I get?
- What do I give?
- Do I belong?
- How can we grow?

These discoveries about workplace engagement led us to ask whether measuring engagement would have the same link to outcomes in congregations that it has in other organizations, although the outcomes are different. We found that when we adapted the measures of engagement to fit faith communities, engagement had just as profound an effect on the outcomes that are relevant to spiritual health. This is because the measures of engagement are human measures — they get to the bottom of the emotional connection between individuals and the organizations to which they belong. And that emotional connection is the key.

This is an important concept that businesses are just now starting to grasp. To relate it to our topic, when it comes to their congregation, members need to "feel" they *get* something of value, they *give* something of value, they *belong*, and they — together with their fellow members — can *grow*. Remember

Jeff and Tricia in Chapter One? What drove their search for a new church home was their quest to rediscover the emotional connection.

CHANGES IN ENGAGEMENT LEVELS

Because engagement is a dynamic process, and is not static, its levels in any church can change. Engaged members can lose their sense of engagement, becoming not-engaged or even actively disengaged. It happens all the time, frequently without leaders' knowledge. Like Tom and Cheryl in Chapter Eight, members don't intentionally set out to become less engaged; more often than not, they just drift into disengagement. To combat this, pay attention to two common causes of the drift toward disengagement.

First, members who no longer have the opportunity to do what they do best find that their engagement level drops. Often, church policy actually encourages this with the "three-year rule," which holds that people can't serve in particular ministry areas for more than three consecutive years. The theory is that this keeps members from becoming burned out and gives the ministry area new blood. But there are two unstated assumptions at work here: One is that church work is so bad that three years is about all anyone can take; the other is that if a committee member isn't a good fit, you have to put up with that person for only three years — after that, he or she is automatically off the team.

I would advocate for something completely different: Recruit people for ministry based on their passions, their God-given talents, and their spiritual gifts, and let them serve in that ministry as long as they are effective. When I was a pastor, we had the three-year rule only when it was legally required by the church's bylaws. For all other ministry areas, we asked people for a one-year commitment, with the opportunity either to move to a different area or to stay with the same one at the end of the year. They could also change ministry areas at any time if their current ministry wasn't working out. This gave people permission to experiment, and find ministry areas in which they could really dig in and grow.

But what about volunteers who aren't productive? What if they're actually hindering the ministry they are attempting to serve? Can you fire volunteers?

Absolutely. If a volunteer is not growing, if his or her service isn't bearing fruit, and if the area of service is suffering, then a leader must "hold up the mirror" and help the volunteer see that the fit isn't right. The volunteer probably already knows this, and the leader is performing a kindness by helping him or her find another area in which to serve. The key is to find a role that fits his or her unique talents — there is most certainly one that's a good match. Remember: Engaged members who are serving in roles they love — and in which they are bearing fruit — do not get burned out. They only get stronger and more energized.

The second cause of a downward drift in engagement is major change. The three biggest changes a church can make are a change in senior pastors (especially if that pastor has been at the church more than 10 years), a change in worship times, and a change in worship styles. Shifts in any or all of these areas disrupt the equilibrium, and during these changes you'll see fewer people strongly agreeing that they know what is expected of them and that their spiritual needs are met.

The departure of a longtime senior pastor, through a move to a new congregation or parish, or retirement, or other factors, can be particularly unsettling for members — even if the transition is a smooth one. The senior pastor is the spiritual leader of the congregation, and members look to him or her for guidance, reassurance, and stability. He or she establishes a certain style and a particular theological interpretation of Scripture, and creates and reflects the culture of the congregation.

When the senior pastor leaves, it raises a lot of questions in parishioners' minds: "Will I like the new pastor's preaching/teaching? Will I still feel like I belong here? What can I expect from the new pastor in terms of pastoral care? Will I like his or her personality? How does this new pastor interpret Scripture?" In a time of transition from one pastor to another, members naturally are not as sure about what is expected of them (or what *to* expect), and they're also not sure whether their spiritual needs will be met.

A change in worship times is more pragmatic than existential, but it is unsettling nonetheless. People are creatures of habit, and when you change their habits, they get nervous. As a hypothetical, let's say that "New Life" church, because of overcrowding in its two worship services — which are now at 9:00 and 10:30 (with Sunday school at 9:00) — decides to add a third service and change the worship times to 8:30, 9:45, and 11:00 — with Sunday school offered at 9:45 and 11:00. If you and your spouse currently attend the 9:00 service — and your kids attend Sunday school at the same time — you've got to change your habits and make a decision, and it's not clear which decision is going to work best for you. If you decide to go to the 8:30 service, you've got to get up earlier (which means getting your kids up earlier), go to worship together, and then go to Sunday school at 9:45, which means you and your spouse will have to find an adult class to attend while the kids are in their classes. Or you could go to the 9:45 service while your kids go to Sunday school, but you'd rather be out of church earlier than 10:45. Do you know what to expect from the new schedule? Will you like it? Will your kids like it? What are the trade-offs?

Changing worship styles is even more unsettling. Let's say that "New Life" is changing not only worship times, but styles as well. It is currently doing traditional Protestant worship at both the 9:00 and 10:30 services — hymns from the hymnal, organ, robed choir, and so on — and is going to make the new 9:45 service a baby-boomer contemporary service, with a band, "lite-rock" praise songs, words projected on screens, worship leaders instead of a choir, and the like. If you've been attending the 9:00 service and are quite happy with the style, now what do you do? Will you like the new service? Will it meet your spiritual needs? What can you expect? What will be expected of you?

Change in the church is never easy, especially when that change is about leadership, habits, and expressions of worship. Engagement can decrease during such times — in fact, it is rare if it doesn't. But if you as a leader follow these two fairly straightforward guidelines in dealing with change, you can lessen the impact it will have on the engagement of your members:

- *Clarify the expectations.* Tell people what they can anticipate — even such seemingly mundane things as the new pastor's office hours, when the "meet and greet" times will be, what the new staff meeting times are, and what the pastor likes to be called. If you are changing worship times and/or styles, indicate what parishioners can expect from the new times and styles of worship, such as what the new traffic flow will be, how many songs will be in the new service, and what new Sunday school classes will be offered. The more you can let people know what to anticipate from the changes, the lower their anxiety levels will be.

- *Communicate!* Whenever you initiate change, relate it to your members early and often. Tell them the reasons for the change, tell them what's coming, and ask for their feedback after the change occurs. Don't ever assume you've done too much communicating; many experts advise that people need to hear something at least three times in at least three different ways before they will understand and remember it. Communication is your best friend when it comes to change.

SPIRITUAL COMMITMENT, ENGAGEMENT, AND OUTCOMES

We've explored in detail how engagement affects outcomes. But does spiritual commitment have an impact as well? Yes. Our research shows a link between spiritual commitment and the four outcomes of life satisfaction, inviting, serving, and giving. Those with higher levels of spiritual commitment are more satisfied with their lives, do more inviting of others to congregational events, spend more time volunteering in their communities, and give more financially to their congregations. So improving spiritual commitment does result in higher outcome scores.

However, on three of the four outcomes — life satisfaction, inviting, and serving — engagement has a relationship that is 3 to 6 times *stronger* than that of spiritual commitment. On giving, engagement has a relationship that is about 1½ times stronger. There are many possible reasons for the relative equality of the effect that engagement and commitment have on giving. One may be that money, like spiritual commitment, is such a personal, individual matter. Sometimes our money represents for us not only our economic status, but our value as people — however misguided that notion may be. Frequently, when individuals have a personal conversion of faith, they reorder their priorities — and that reordering includes their finances.

Michael's story is representative of such a change. Michael was regular in his attendance at Mass at St. Gerard Majella, the church described in Chapter Seven, but whenever the priests would preach on money, he would get irritated. "I don't come to church for this!" he thought. "I come to pray with my family and friends in our church community, listen to the Scriptures and the Word of God, and perhaps catch a good sermon that would give me some insight as to how I should be living my life. Do I have to be subject to these incessant requests for money? Besides, I don't have any. I give what I can each week. Why won't they leave us alone already?" Things finally came to a head for Michael, and one week when the priest started talking about money, he got up in the middle of the service and walked out.

Things weren't going well in Michael's personal life. As he tells it, "I had reached a time of my life when everything seemed dismal. As I lay in bed, crying myself to sleep each night, I kept praying that things would get better. I was out of work, out of money, my mortgage payment and bills kept coming, and I was struggling to provide for my family's basic needs. I literally didn't have much else to lose. I felt as if I had absolutely no control over my life. I finally cracked."

It dawned on Michael that his prayers were "Give me this!" or "Send me that!" — always asking for something to get his life back on course. He came to the conclusion that he needed a different approach. "I decided that I would admit to God that my life was in his control, not mine," Michael recalls. "It was obvious that I had no control over it. I told God that I would do whatever he wanted, if he would only show me the way."

He soon realized that he was missing the big picture. The focus of his life was misdirected. "Here I was worrying about the day-to-day details of my life (my worries, bills, appointments, etc.) and I wasn't focusing on the only thing that really matters: My relationship with God, and my quest for salvation."

From that point on, Michael made a conscious effort to focus his energy on the true goal: "doing what God has asked us to do here on earth — be his ambassadors, evangelize, and spread the Word of God."

These events shaped the way he felt about money and the church. "I was aware that the things I owned, however great or small, were parts of my responsibility," he says. "Putting God in control of my life was only the start. I needed to give of myself fully." So from the miniscule amount of money he was receiving at the time from unemployment checks, he decided to give a portion to the church, hoping that what he had always heard was true: That God would provide.

Now, a few years later, Michael is a leader in his church and one of the most vocal advocates of stewardship principles. And he also discovered that God indeed would provide — though not with a "handout." Through his renewed faith, Michael found the courage to start his own business, which is now thriving. Because of his growing engagement in his church, Michael is a happier and spiritually healthier person.

It's an inspiring story, and in Michael's case, his deepened spiritual commitment led to an increase in his giving. But it tends to be more common for strengthened engagement to lead to increased giving — and definitely more common for engagement to lead to increases in the other three relevant outcomes.

If you were to diagram the effect that engagement and commitment have on outcomes, it would look like this:

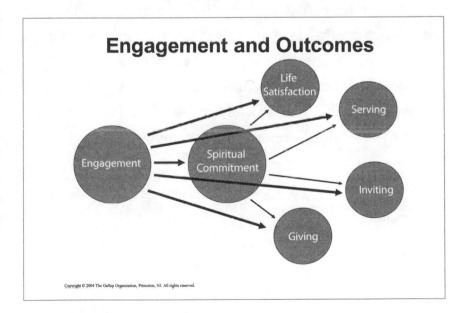

The impact of spiritual commitment is represented by the thin arrows; that of engagement is represented by the thicker arrows. In addition, our research shows that there is evidence of a causal, not just corollary, relationship between engagement and commitment.

But one of the main reasons I recommend focusing on engagement is that it's more actionable than commitment. That is, you can take more achievable, concrete steps to help your congregation improve its engagement level than you can to increase its spiritual commitment. For example, how are you going to ensure that your members' faith is involved in every aspect of their lives? What action plans will you make? It would be difficult at best to do. But you can create actionable strategies and plans to ensure that members are clear about the expectations of membership, or that they have the opportunity to do what they do best, or that someone talks to them about the progress of their spiritual growth at least once every six months.

That's why engagement is more actionable. And if you take action on the items that measure engagement, increased spiritual commitment will almost assuredly follow.

Chapter Ten:
Preparing the Soil

ithin two months of its grand opening celebration, Huntington Ridge Retirement Center had a waiting list. The need for such a center in its community is great, and Huntington Ridge is the type of facility where one could move from independent living in an apartment to assisted living, and then to a full-time skilled nursing facility, all within the same complex. The food served in the dining room is first-rate, there are abundant activities, and the nursing care is exceptional. Seniors from a four-state region move in to Huntington Ridge when living in their own homes becomes too much of a burden, and the great majority of new residents are delighted to be there.

"Northside Church" is Huntington Ridge's closest neighbor, and its pastor, leaders, and members watched with great interest as the vast complex was being built. Northside is also a church with a high percentage of engaged members. Among other things, most of the members would say they know what is expected of them; that their opinions count; that in their congregation, they regularly have the opportunity to do what they do best; and that the spiritual leaders care about them as individuals.

Northside's leadership is constantly thinking about new ways in which the church's members can live out their faith in service to others. "Every member in ministry — that's our goal," says Pastor Davis, who has been the senior pastor of Northside for about nine years. Twice a month, members of the church lead worship services at Huntington Ridge, and many of the residents consider Northside their church home.

Shortly after Huntington Ridge opened, a member of Northside Church, Lisa, decided that the retirement center would become her "mission field" — especially the skilled nursing center. Lisa had been trying to figure out just what her ministry would be, and this seemed to be the right fit with her talents, life experience, and interests. So she started making regular visits to Huntington Ridge, getting to know the staff and visiting the residents — paying particular attention to residents who didn't seem to have much family around. Lisa would befriend them, and her joyful countenance brought light and life to some whose lives would otherwise have been painted in shades of gray. The staff always looked forward to Lisa's visits, because they knew how much her presence meant to their patients. Lisa also would keep Pastor Davis and other church leaders informed of any pastoral needs the residents had.

One day the head nurse at the center approached Lisa as she came to visit residents. "Lisa, do you have a minute?" she asked. "I need to talk to you about one of our newest residents. She just moved in a couple of days ago, and I'm really concerned." The head nurse proceeded to tell Lisa about Brigitte.

Brigitte had no family, and no friends that anyone knew of — it seems she had outlived them. She had moved into the skilled nursing center of Huntington Ridge from the retirement side.

Brigitte had come to the United States from Germany — her husband, Frank, was a U.S. soldier she met and married while he was stationed in Germany shortly after World War II. Brigitte and Frank had no children, and she never quite got comfortable with English. They had had a good life together, and when they could no longer keep up their house and Brigitte got sick, they decided to move into the Huntington Ridge retirement center.

Less than a month after Brigitte and Frank moved into their apartment, Frank died of a sudden heart attack. Brigitte was battling cancer and could no longer stay in her apartment, so she moved into the skilled nursing center.

Not long after she started living there, the staff was concerned because Brigitte was depressed — never venturing from her room, never speaking to anyone, eating hardly anything at all, just sitting in her wheelchair staring out the window.

"Would you please stop by and see her?" the head nurse asked Lisa. "If anybody can bring Brigitte out of her shell, it would be you."

"I don't know about that," replied Lisa, "but I'll do what I can."

When she got to Brigitte's room, Lisa found her just as the head nurse described: despondent and unresponsive. She barely made eye contact with Lisa, and said not a word to her. "Brigitte, I'll be back tomorrow to see you, would that be OK?" Lisa asked on her way out of the room. To Lisa's surprise, Brigitte nodded. "I'll see you tomorrow, then," Lisa said brightly as she left the room. "Good-bye, Brigitte!" She was determined to find a way to reach Brigitte and bring her back to life.

On subsequent visits, things got a little better. Lisa brought Brigitte an African violet plant, and also would read to her from the newspaper and her church's daily devotional book. Brigitte still did not say much more than "hello" and "good-bye," but she would make eye contact with Lisa. Yet she seemed to be getting frailer and was still depressed.

After one such visit, Lisa had an idea, and she shared it with Colleen, the Northside Church gifts coordinator. "Colleen," she asked, "do you know anybody in our congregation who speaks German?" And she proceeded to tell Colleen about Brigitte.

"Hmm. I think I might know someone who would be perfect for this," said Colleen. "Give me a couple of days and I will see what I can do. Brigitte really needs us, doesn't she?"

"Yes she does," replied Lisa.

Because of her position as gifts coordinator and her commitment to helping people find the right fit in ministry, there were few people who knew more about the members of Northside than Colleen did. She remembered that one of their retired members, Margaret, had come to the United States from Germany when she was a small girl. Colleen approached Margaret about Brigitte's situation.

"I'll certainly give it a try," said Margaret. "My German is a little rusty — I haven't used it much in the 20 years since my mother died. It will give me an excuse to become fluent again!"

Two days later, Lisa and Margaret went to visit Brigitte.

"Brigitte," said Lisa, "I have someone I'd like you to meet. This is Margaret."

"*Guten Morgen, Brigitte,*" said Margaret. "*Wie geht es Ihnen heute?*" (Good morning, Brigitte. How are you today?)

Brigitte looked up. Her eyes widened. And a delighted smile spread across her face.

"*Ich bin wunderbar jetzt! Vielen Dank, daß Sie gekommen sind!*" (I am wonderful now! Thank you for coming!) And so began a conversation in German between Brigitte and Margaret that went on for nearly an hour and a half. Margaret had to ask for help every so often, but Brigitte was more than happy to oblige. Lisa looked on in amazement at the transformation taking place before her eyes.

Through Margaret, Lisa found out that Brigitte very much wanted to take communion, but hadn't been able to since she moved into the care center. Lisa relayed the information, and Pastor Davis began to make weekly visits to Brigitte to fulfill her wish.

In the two months that followed, as Margaret made nearly daily visits to Brigitte, the care staff noticed a remarkable change in her. She began eating more, she started smiling again, and even started using her walker to get around the halls of the center and visit other residents. The staff and other residents came to deeply appreciate Brigitte's twinkling eyes, sparkling smile, and joy of life.

But Brigitte knew that she was fighting a losing battle with cancer, and soon the cancer started winning. Eventually she was confined to her bed, and in her final days the pain medication made it hard for her to stay awake much of the time.

On one of his last visits to Brigitte, as Pastor Davis was giving her communion, she took his hand and said, "Thank you so much, pastor. Your church, your people saved my life."

Brigitte died three days later, peacefully in her sleep. Those who knew her in her last days remember her not as the lonely, depressed woman they first met at the care center, but as a delightful soul who brought joy and happiness into the lives of all whom she met.

I share this story with you to illustrate how committed, passionate people in a congregation can deeply affect other people's lives, and change them for the better. And that, ultimately, is what you and I are trying to do here: We are trying to change lives.

After Jesus' death and resurrection, the Apostle Paul gave his life (after his conversion to Christianity) to planting new churches in the Hellenic world — even going as far as Rome itself in his missionary journeys. Any astute reader can see in his letters Paul's fervent hopes and dreams for the churches he planted. He was constantly looking for ways to encourage, correct, and mentor the Christians in these churches, for he knew beyond a doubt that local churches were the hope of the world.

Paul spent time in prison, was beaten, and shipwrecked. He even parted ways with the Jerusalem church leaders. Paul did all of this so that he could be faithful to his calling from God to plant and grow thriving churches that would witness to the lifesaving, life-giving power of God's love poured out for humanity in the life, death, and resurrection of Jesus. And Paul wound up dying a martyr's death, like most of the rest of the Apostles and disciples, for his faith — a faith that found its embodiment in the Church.

Because we are "surrounded by so great a cloud of witnesses," can we do less than give our best for the advancement of the Church? Can we do less than see to it that every member and potential member has the opportunity to — and is invited to — become engaged in our local churches? I believe we have no higher calling as leaders in the Church of Jesus Christ. We can help the Church *be* the Church once again.

Help your church to become an engaged congregation. Prepare the soil so that God can do amazing things in your midst. Because people like those you've met in this book — the Jeffs and the Tricias, the Jennifers, the Alexes, the Roberts, the Michaels, the Lisas, and the Brigittes — are counting on it.

LEARN MORE

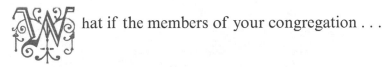hat if the members of your congregation . . .

- were *13 times* more likely to have invited someone to participate in your church in the past month?

- were *three times* as satisfied with their lives?

- spent *more than two hours per week* serving and helping others in their communities?

- *tripled* their giving to your church?

To learn how Gallup can put the power of engagement to work in your congregation, or for more information on Gallup Faith, please contact us at 1-800-288-8592 or engagedchurches@gallup.com, or log on to our Web site at www.gallupfaith.com.

To take your leadership to the next level and become a truly world-class leader, investigate Gallup Faith's Leadership Excellence program at www.gallupfaith.com.

Appendix A

OVERVIEW

Since its inception, The Gallup Organization has had a long history of interest in and research directed toward religion, spirituality, and the faith of the American people. Building on a tradition of research into these areas, the Gallup Faith Poll and Congregational Engagement Index were launched in the fall of 2001.

This appendix provides details regarding the development and fielding of the annual Gallup Faith Poll, while Appendix B describes the development and efficacy of the Congregational Engagement Index.

Each year, Gallup conducts telephone interviews with approximately 1,000 adults (aged 18 and older) who indicate that they are members of a church, synagogue, or other religious faith community. Beginning in 2002, Gallup added a nonmember component to its sample design, conducting interviews with approximately 500 adults (aged 18 and older) who report that they are *not* members of a church, synagogue, or other faith community. This member-to-nonmember ratio approximates estimates of the proportion of religious group members to nonmembers in the U.S. population in general (Gallup Poll).

During the 10-minute English-language telephone interview, respondents are asked to rate their agreement or disagreement with a number of items designed to gauge an individual's level of spiritual commitment and congregational engagement. Outcome constructs like life satisfaction, giving, serving, and inviting, as well as general demographic information, are also collected from respondents. [See Table 3.0 for a full list of items common to all administrations of the Gallup Faith Poll.]

DATA COLLECTION

Data for the Gallup Faith Poll were collected in the fall of each year, 2001 through 2005, with approximately one month allotted for all data-collection activities during each annual iteration. Interviews were conducted via telephone by trained professional interviewing staff members, using a five-call design. Households were called between the hours of 5:00 p.m. and 9:30 p.m. (in respondents' time zones), to ensure the inclusion of working adults in the participant pool.

To improve interviewer consistency, CATI (Computer-Assisted Telephone Interviewing) technology was employed and staff members were regularly briefed on details of the study. Within each household, respondent selection was based on the adult in the household who had celebrated his or her birthday most recently. Interviews were conducted in English only.

RESPONSE RATE

The CASRO response rates for the annual Gallup Faith Polls conducted in 2001 through 2005 ranged from 23% to 26%, with an average response rate across all years of 24%. This means Gallup was able to complete interviews with nearly one-quarter of all eligible and presumed eligible households that were randomly selected for inclusion in the study. Table 1.0 details the number of religious group members and nonmembers surveyed for each year of the poll, and provides the CASRO response rate for each iteration of the study.

Table 1.0 — Response Rate by Year

Year	Members	Nonmembers	CASRO Response Rate
2001	1,006	*	26%
2002	1,000	501	23%
2003	1,002	500	25%
2004	1,000	500	**
2005	1,001	502	23%

*Nonmembers were not included in 2001 Gallup Faith Poll.
**CASRO response rate unavailable for 2004 Gallup Faith Poll.

RESPONDENT CHARACTERISTICS

Prior to weighting, the characteristics of Gallup Faith Poll respondents were analyzed to determine whether any significant changes in respondent demographics had occurred. Any changes were assessed as potential sources of bias.

Just as response rates remained relatively stable, unweighted respondent demographic characteristics did not vary much across the five years.

Respondent Age

As Table 2.1 indicates, average age fluctuated slightly, but remained in the 47- to 51-year range for all years of the study.

Table 2.1 — Average Respondent Age by Year

Year	Mean Age	Standard Deviation
2001	49.7 yrs	17.9
2002	47.0 yrs	17.5
2003	48.1 yrs	16.8
2004	48.1 yrs	17.4
2005	50.8 yrs	17.2

Respondent Gender

The Gallup Faith Poll gender mix remained relatively consistent, with approximately 60% females and 40% males comprising each year's respondent group. See Table 2.2 for annual gender statistics.

Table 2.2 — Respondent Gender by Year

Year	Male	Female
2001	40.2%	59.8%
2002	39.2%	60.8%
2003	40.9%	59.1%
2004	36.7%	63.3%
2005	37.7%	62.3%

Race/Ethnicity

While the percentage of respondents answering "Other"/ "Don't know"/"Refused" to questions about race and ethnicity increased slightly, from 4% in 2001 to highs of around 7%, the racial distribution as a whole remained relatively steady. As Table 2.3 details, the respondent pool has typically been composed of approximately 80% white respondents, 10% African-American respondents, and 3%-5% Hispanic respondents.

Table 2.3 — Respondent Race/Ethnicity by Year

Year	White	African-American	Hispanic	Other/DK/Ref
2001	83.4%	9.3%	3.6%	3.7%
2002	77.5%	9.8%	5.5%	7.2%
2003	82.4%	8.3%	3.3%	6.0%
2004	78.6%	9.9%	4.5%	7.0%
2005	80.8%	10.2%	3.4%	5.6%

Marital Status

The percentage of single respondents increased slightly over the five years of the study, while the percentage of widowed participants decreased, leaving a mix of study participants that was approximately 60% married, 20% single, 10% divorced/separated, and 8% widowed (see Table 2.4).

Table 2.4 — Respondent Marital Status by Year

Year	Married	Single	Divorced/Separated	Widowed
2001	58.4%	17.8%	10.8%	12.5%
2002	55.0%	24.9%	9.2%	7.9%
2003	56.6%	21.9%	11.8%	8.3%
2004	54.7%	20.4%	10.0%	7.7%
2005	58.8%	19.6%	10.1%	7.9%

Education

Educational attainment among Gallup Faith Poll participants remained stable between 2001 and 2005, with approximately 30% of respondents reporting a high school diploma or less as their highest level of education, and 40% reporting attainment of a college degree or postgraduate work/degree, as Table 2.5 details.

Table 2.5 — Respondent Educational Attainment by Year

Year	High School/Less	Trade/Tech/Vocational/Some College	College Graduate	Postgraduate Work/Degree
2001	31.8%	27.8%	24.2%	16.0%
2002	33.3%	25.3%	25.3%	13.1%
2003	31.4%	25.3%	26.4%	15.5%
2004	31.1%	20.6%	26.5%	14.3%
2005	29.9%	26.1%	22.6%	17.5%

Income and Occupation

Levels of self-reported total annual household income (see Table 2.6) and the distribution across occupational categories (see Table 2.7) shifted slightly over the years, but respondents most commonly fit into the $40,000 to $60,000 annual household income level, and were most likely to report occupations that were professional/managerial (30%), services/labor (14%), or homemaker (10%). In all years, retired/disabled participants represented around one-fifth of the respondent pool.

Table 2.6 — Respondent Total Annual Household Income Level by Year

Year	<$10K	$10K-<$20K	$20K-<$30K	$30K-<$40K	$40K-<$60K	$60K-<$75K	$75K-<$100K	$100K+
2001	7.3%	11.1%	11.0%	11.1%	16.8%	10.0%	8.3%	10.8%
2002	4.7%	13.3%	10.0%	10.9%	14.3%	7.5%	7.4%	9.7%
2003	4.9%	10.7%	10.3%	12.2%	18.2%	9.1%	10.7%	13.5%
2004	6.0%	9.0%	8.1%	9.9%	12.5%	8.5%	9.0%	11.4%
2005	4.9%	8.8%	10.4%	8.3%	12.5%	8.7%	8.3%	10.9%

Table 2.7 — Respondent Occupation by Year

Occupation	Year 2001	2002	2003	2004	2005
Professional/Managerial	30.4%	29.8%	31.4%	30.9%	29.5%
Services/Labor	16.2%	14.5%	14.7%	12.7%	12.2%
Homemaker	8.8%	8.8%	9.3%	7.7%	9.8%
Secretarial/Clerical	5.6%	4.7%	6.3%	6.4%	5.1%
Sales/Retail Sales	4.1%	5.1%	5.3%	4.5%	5.3%
Self-Employed	3.0%	3.3%	2.9%	3.4%	3.7%
Farmer/Rancher	0.7%	0.5%	0.6%	0.5%	0.5%
Military	0.4%	0.6%	0.6%	0.7%	0.7%
Other	0.7%	--	1.5%	0.1%	0.3%
Retired/Disabled	23.6%	20.9%	20.1%	18.3%	23.0%
Student	4.1%	4.3%	2.8%	2.7%	1.4%
Unemployed	1.7%	4.0%	2.9%	3.9%	4.1%

Religious Affiliation

Gallup's random sampling of adults in the United States did not detect major changes in religious group affiliation across the years. However, participants who reported membership in the Roman Catholic Church fell from 25% in 2001 to 17% in 2005 (see Table 2.8). Further study is necessary to determine whether this observation was because of a sampling anomaly, or is the indication of a trend.

Table 2.8 — Respondent Religious Affiliation by Year

Religious Affiliation*	Year				
	2001	2002	2003	2004	2005
Protestant	65.0%	66.2%	62.7%	61.9%	63.8%
Roman Catholic	25.3%	21.6%	23.7%	20.2%	17.2%
Other	8.3%	7.5%	10.5%	7.1%	11.5%
Agnostic/ None/DK/Ref	1.4%	4.7%	3.1%	10.8%	7.5%

*Nonmembers excluded from this analysis for 2002-2005 survey administrations.

WEIGHTING

Once collected, the respondents' data were weighted to adjust for unequal probabilities of inclusion because of variation in the number of adults present in each selected household, nonresponse bias because of unequal cooperation rates, and sample stratification by self-identified religious group "members" vs. "nonmembers."

The number of adults present in each participant's household was used to adjust for the unequal probability of inclusion, while the respondents' particular demographic characteristics were adjusted to match U.S. Census Bureau demographic estimates in order to mitigate the impact of nonresponse bias. Cases were then weighted to ensure that the proportion of religious group members to nonmembers approximated that of the general population. Once these factors had been incorporated into the weighting scheme, a final adjustment was made so that the total weighted number of responses was equal to the actual number of participants in the study.

Conceptually, the weighting formula employed was:

[Household Wt] * [Ethnicity Wt] * [Race Wt] *
[AgeGrp Wt] * [Gender Wt] * [Member Wt]

APPLICATIONS OF DATA

The results of this study are intended to be generalizable to the contiguous (excluding Alaska and Hawaii) United States English-speaking, non-institutionalized adult population with telephone access. Individuals who were in institutions (including hospitals, prisons, and treatment centers) at the time of each study iteration were not represented by that iteration's sample frame.

This questionnaire was administered via telephone in English only; individuals who were uncomfortable communicating or unable to communicate in English and those who were unable to communicate via telephone were not studied. On average, approximately 2% of households contacted for inclusion in the study were unable to participate because of a hearing or language barrier.

Adults aged 18 and older were eligible for inclusion in this study; members of generations who were younger than 18 years of age at the time of a given administration were not eligible for the study at that time. Thus, inasmuch as there *may be a potential* for generational differences in religiosity, spirituality, and congregational engagement, longitudinal trends will need to examine the potential impact of cohort differences on these constructs.

The sample frame for this study is designed to provide estimations for the general United States population. With an approximate total annual sample size of 1,500 respondents, adequate sample does not exist to make generalizations about groups that comprise a small proportion of the United States population. In general, conclusions specific to religious groups, racial and ethnic groups, and other data segmentations that comprise less than 10% of the U.S. population cannot be drawn from these data.

— Julie K. Hawkins
The Gallup Organization

Table 3.0 — Items Common to All Gallup Faith Poll Administrations

Congregational Engagement Items

As a member of my congregation/parish, I know what is expected of me.

In my congregation/parish, my spiritual needs are met.

In my congregation/parish, I regularly have the opportunity to do what I do best.

In the last month, I have received recognition or praise from someone in my congregation/parish.

The spiritual leaders in my congregation/parish seem to care about me as a person.

There is someone in my congregation/parish who encourages my spiritual development.

As a member of my congregation/parish, my opinions seem to count.

The mission or purpose of my congregation/parish makes me feel my participation is important.

The other members of my congregation/parish are committed to spiritual growth.

Aside from family members, I have a best friend in my congregation/parish.

In the last six months, someone in my congregation/parish has talked to me about the progress of my spiritual growth.

In my congregation/parish, I have opportunities to learn and grow.

Spiritual Commitment Items

My faith is involved in every aspect of my life.

Because of my faith, I have meaning and purpose in my life.

My faith gives me an inner peace.

I am a person who is spiritually committed.

I spend time in worship or prayer every day.

Because of my faith, I have forgiven people who have hurt me deeply.

My faith has called me to develop my given strengths.

I will take unpopular stands to defend my faith.

I speak words of kindness to those in need of encouragement.

Outcomes

I am completely satisfied with my life.

In the last month, I have invited someone to participate in my congregation/parish.

Thinking about the amount of money you give to your congregation/parish, would you say you give more than 10% or less than 10% of your income each year?

How much do you give to your congregation annually?

On average, how many volunteer hours a week do you give to help and serve others in your community?

Demographics

Please tell me your age.

Gender

Are you, yourself, of Hispanic origin or descent, such as Mexican, Puerto Rican, Cuban, or other Spanish background?

What is your race? Are you white, African American, Asian, or some other race?

If "Hispanic" answer given to either ethnicity or race question:
Do you consider yourself to be white-Hispanic, or black-Hispanic?

What is your religious preference?

Including parents and children, how many people are in your household?

What is your marital status?

What is the highest level of education you have completed?

What is your current occupation?

Total annual household income

APPENDIX B

CONGREGATIONAL ENGAGEMENT INDEX

A portion of the Gallup Faith Poll is designed to measure an individual's self-reported level of congregational engagement. When considered in total, the congregational engagement items are intended to assess how strongly an individual feels a sense of belonging within his or her religious organization. *Only members of a church, synagogue, or other religious faith group are eligible for congregational engagement assessment.*

Congregational engagement spans four thematic areas:
- What do I get?
- What do I give?
- Do I belong?
- How can we grow?

Development — Items that comprise the Gallup Congregational Engagement Index battery were selected through a pretesting process. Data for the pretest were collected in October 2000 using a three-call design, using Computer-Assisted Telephone Interviewing (CATI). Selection for the study was based on youngest male/oldest female in each household.

Pretest participants (n=700) were asked 14 items selected for their conceptual ability to assess the four subthemes of congregational engagement. Based upon statistical analyses, these 14 items were reduced and refined to the 12 most efficient measures of congregational engagement.

Operationalization — Participants were asked to report their level of agreement or disagreement with each of the following statements, using a 5-point scale where "5" means strongly agree and "1" means strongly disagree.

CONGREGATIONAL ENGAGEMENT: WHAT DO I GET?

- As a member of my congregation/parish, I know what is expected of me.
- In my congregation/parish, my spiritual needs are met.

CONGREGATIONAL ENGAGEMENT: WHAT DO I GIVE?

- In my congregation/parish, I regularly have the opportunity to do what I do best.
- In the last month, I have received recognition or praise from someone in my congregation/parish.
- The spiritual leaders in my congregation/parish seem to care about me as a person.
- There is someone in my congregation/parish who encourages my spiritual development.

CONGREGATIONAL ENGAGEMENT: DO I BELONG?

- As a member of my congregation/parish, my opinions seem to count.
- The mission or purpose of my congregation/parish makes me feel my participation is important.
- The other members of my congregation/parish are committed to spiritual growth.
- Aside from family members, I have a best friend in my congregation/parish.

CONGREGATIONAL ENGAGEMENT: HOW CAN WE GROW?

- In the last six months, someone in my congregation/parish has talked to me about the progress of my spiritual growth.
- In my congregation/parish, I have opportunities to learn and grow.

Respondents must answer 10 or more of these items in order to receive a congregational engagement composite score. "Don't know" and "Refused" responses are considered nonresponsive and discarded from consideration. Responses to these 10 to 12 items are then summarized to derive each participant's congregational engagement composite mean score.

Next, each individual's composite score is compared to critical index values in order to categorize each person's level of engagement with his or her respective congregation as "engaged" "not-engaged" or "actively disengaged." A proprietary formula, developed by The Gallup Organization, is used to classify each respondent into one of these engagement categories.

Development of this proprietary formula was based upon the relationship of engagement items to participants' life satisfaction, inviting, serving, and giving. Initial critical index values were set by examining the impact that respondents' engagement had on these important outcome variables.

CONGREGATIONAL ENGAGEMENT INDEX SCALE PERFORMANCE

The Congregational Engagement Index demonstrates internal consistency (Cronbach's Alpha=0.917) and has been shown to correlate with self-reported outcome variables, including participants' general life satisfaction ($r=0.288$, $p<.05$), community volunteerism ($r=0.181$, $p<.05$), financial contributions to participants' religious congregations ($r=0.256$, $p<.05$), and inviting others to attend religious services ($r=0.505$, $p<.05$).

Each of the 12 items included in the Congregational Engagement Index scale shows a strong relationship to the scale itself, indicating that the items may indeed be measuring one underlying construct. The data suggest that this construct may be better measured by the combined 12 items in scale form rather than any of the 12 individual items. Examination of Item-Scale statistics points to no items that should be removed from the scale, as Table 4.0 details.

Table 4.0 — Item-Scale Statistics

Item	Corrected Item-Total Correlation	Squared Multiple Correlation	Cronbach's Alpha if Item Deleted
As a member of my congregation/parish, I know what is expected of me.	0.572	0.409	0.914
In my congregation/parish, my spiritual needs are met.	0.691	0.559	0.909
In my congregation/parish, I regularly have the opportunity to do what I do best.	0.673	0.507	0.909
In the last month, I have received recognition or praise from someone in my congregation/parish.	0.622	0.423	0.913
The spiritual leaders in my congregation/parish seem to care about me as a person.	0.736	0.586	0.907
There is someone in my congregation/parish who encourages my spiritual development.	0.759	0.594	0.905
As a member of my congregation/parish, my opinions seem to count.	0.776	0.657	0.905
The mission or purpose of my congregation/parish makes me feel my participation is important.	0.797	0.691	0.904
The other members of my congregation/parish are committed to spiritual growth.	0.586	0.382	0.913
Aside from family members, I have a best friend in my congregation/parish.	0.583	0.366	0.915
In the last six months, someone in my congregation/parish has talked to me about the progress of my spiritual growth.	0.602	0.434	0.915
In my congregation/parish, I have opportunities to learn and grow.	.0703	0.560	0.907

— Julie K. Hawkins
The Gallup Organization

ACKNOWLEDGEMENTS

There are a multitude of individuals who contribute to the successful completion of any book; this one is no exception. I owe a debt of gratitude to the following individuals:

To Jim Clifton, Chairman and CEO of The Gallup Organization, whose original vision for the Faith Communities Practice was to build a metric that was Web-based, scalable, and global — and then to write a book on it. Also to Larry Emond, for his encouragement and belief in my talent and ability to lead this endeavor.

To Jim Harter and Julie Hawkins, whose analysis, expertise, and creativity gave shape, form, and measurement to what was in the beginning just another good idea. And to the late Dr. Donald O. Clifton, one of the best question-writers the research world has ever known.

To Geoff Brewer, Paul Petters, Darren Carlson, Mark Stiemann, and Julie Ray for their editing prowess — you all make me sound smarter and more eloquent than I actually am. To Molly Hardin, who created the book's elegant and sophisticated design. To Piotrek Juszkiewicz for his expert attention to the myriad details — both large and small

— involved in publishing this book; and to Rachel Johanowicz, for managing the production processes with grace and flawless execution.

To Joe Cavanaugh, Cinda Hicks, and Cassi Warren for keeping the needs of the market clearly in mind. Also to Curt Coffman, Dennis Welch, Scott Simmons, Tim Dean, Tim Simon, Scott Wright, Brian Dawson, and a host of other Gallup associates — both past and present — who helped create, design, and promote the ME[25].

To Fr. Bill Hanson and Fr. Chris Heller and the members of the Church of St. Gerard Majella, Port Jefferson Station, New York — especially Marie Guido and Michael Cook. Thank you for allowing me the privilege of journeying with you on the road toward engagement. And to the Rev. Tony Dawson and the members of St. Andrew's United Methodist Church, Omaha, Nebraska: being your founding pastor was a once-in-a-lifetime experience. "Thank you" doesn't begin to say it all!

To Leonard Sweet for a great day on Orcas Island, reviewing the initial draft, and sharing valuable insights.

To the panel participants who reviewed early drafts of this book and gave valuable feedback.

Finally, and most importantly, to my wife, Jane, and daughters, Julie and Kaleigh — thank you for your love and support through the years, and especially in this project.

Thank you all.

ABOUT THE AUTHOR

Al Winseman is Global Practice Leader for Faith-Based Organizations for The Gallup Organization, and consults with congregations, denominations, and other religious organizations across the country, helping them put the power of engagement to work to improve their effectiveness. He is a co-author of *Living Your Strengths*, written to help members of congregations discover and use their God-given talents and strengths.

Prior to joining Gallup, Winseman served as a pastor in the United Methodist Church for 15 years. He lives in Lincoln, Nebraska, with his wife, Jane, and their two college-aged daughters, Julie and Kaleigh.

Gallup Press exists to educate and inform the people who govern, manage, teach, and lead the world's six billion citizens. Each book meets The Gallup Organization's requirements of integrity, trust, and independence and is based on Gallup-approved science and research.